dinner with friends

Published in 2007 by Murdoch Books Pty Limited.
www.murdochbooks.com.au

Murdoch Books Australia
Pier 8/9, 23 Hickson Road
Millers Point NSW 2000
Phone: + 61 (0) 2 8220 2000
Fax: + 61 (0) 2 8220 2558

Murdoch Books UK Limited
Erico House, 6th Floor
93–99 Upper Richmond Road
Putney, London SW15 2TG
Phone: + 44 (0) 20 8785 5995
Fax: + 44 (0) 20 8785 5985

Chief Executive: Juliet Rogers
Publishing Director: Kay Scarlett

Design Manager: Vivien Valk
Concept & Art Direction: Sarah Odgers
Design: Jacqueline Duncan
Project Manager and Editor: Rhiain Hull
Production: Monika Paratore
Photographer: Jared Fowler
Stylist: Cherise Koch
Food preparation: Alan Wilson
Introduction text: Leanne Kitchen
Recipes developed by the Murdoch Books Test Kitchen

National Library of Australia Cataloguing-in-Publication Data
Dinner with friends. Includes index.
ISBN 978 1 74045 903 7. ISBN 1 74045 903 2.
1. Dinners and dining 2. Cookery I. Price, Jane (Jane Paula Wynn).
II. Title. (Series: Kitchen Classics; 2). 641.54

A catalogue record for this book is available from the British Library

Printed by 1010 Printing International Limited in 2007. PRINTED IN CHINA.
Reprinted 2007 (three times).

CONVERSION GUIDE: You may find cooking times vary depending on the oven you are using. For fan-forced ovens, as a general rule, set the oven temperature to 20°C (35°F) lower than indicated in the recipe. We have used 20 ml (4 teaspoon) tablespoon measures. If you are using a 15 ml (3 teaspoon) tablespoon, for most recipes the difference will not be noticeable. However, for recipes using baking powder, gelatine, bicarbonate of soda (baking soda), small amounts of flour, add an extra teaspoon for each tablespoon specified.

dinner with friends

THE ENTERTAINING RECIPES YOU MUST HAVE

SERIES EDITOR **JANE PRICE**

MURDOCH BOOKS

CONTENTS

THE COMPANY OF FRIENDS

For those of us who love to cook, there are few pleasures in life greater than having friends over for dinner. Oh, sure — it's lovely to go to a restaurant, select dishes from an artfully crafted menu and have them served by polished professionals but, when we invite people into our own home and treat them to food we've cooked and drinks we've chosen ourselves, the dining experience becomes even more gratifying.

Dinner parties these days can be as laid-back as you like and involve nothing more formal than guests draping themselves over outdoor furniture, enjoying casual fare like barbecued octopus, citrus and avocado salad and asparagus vinaigrette served on paper plates. At the other end of the spectrum, hosting a dinner party can be an excellent opportunity to dust off crystal glasses and special flatware, to raid the wine cellar and put together swish food to match; think seafood terrine, rack of lamb with herb crust and chocolate and cinnamon ice cream. However food is served, it's imperative that the various dishes complement each other and are appropriate to the occasion. There's unquestionably a knack to getting the balance right and in *Dinner with Friends*, this has been made simple. Here you'll find all the recipes you need to plan any dinner party menu, from starters, centre-stage meat and fish dishes, vegetable accompaniments and refreshing salads through to grand-finale desserts. Each chapter is organized around a theme — 'Elegant', 'Summer', 'Winter', 'Mediterranean', and 'Asian' — so every season and inclination of the cook is accommodated. Within each chapter, recipes have been chosen with mixing and matching in mind, so you can not only design your own menus but have endless combinations of dishes up your sleeve for many future occasions.

ELEGANT ENTERTAINING

HERB PANCAKES WITH AVOCADO BUTTER

60 g (2¼ oz/½ cup) plain
(all-purpose) flour
60 g (2¼ oz/½ cup) self-raising flour
1 egg, lightly beaten
125 ml (4 fl oz/½ cup) milk
4 tablespoons finely chopped mixed
herbs

AVOCADO BUTTER
½ avocado
60 g (2¼ oz) butter
1 tablespoon lemon or lime juice

MAKES ABOUT 50

Sift the flours into a large bowl and make a well in the centre. In a separate bowl, combine the egg, milk, herbs and 1 teaspoon cracked black pepper and gradually add to the flour, whisking until the batter is smooth and free of lumps.

Heat a frying pan and brush with melted butter. Drop teaspoons of batter into the pan and cook until bubbles appear on top. Turn and cook until golden underneath. Keep warm while you repeat with the rest of the batter.

To make the avocado butter, mix the avocado, butter, lemon or lime juice and ½ teaspoon cracked black pepper in a small bowl until smooth, then spread over the pancakes. Garnish with cracked black pepper and serve.

PREPARATION TIME: 30 MINUTES   COOKING TIME: 30 MINUTES

SMOKED FISH PÂTÉ

4 smoked mackerel or smoked trout fillets
2–3 tablespoons lemon or lime juice
125 g (4½ oz/½ cup) cream cheese,
softened
200 g (7 oz) butter, melted
herb sprigs (for example, dill, fennel,
flat-leaf (Italian) parsley), to garnish
lemon slices, to garnish

SERVES 4–6

Remove the skin and bones from the fish and roughly flake the flesh. Put the flesh in a blender or food processor with the lemon or lime juice, cream cheese and butter. Blend or process until smooth. Season with pepper to taste.

Spread into a 500 ml (17 fl oz/2-cup) serving dish and chill for several hours. Garnish with sprigs of fresh herbs and lemon slices. Serve with melba toast or crackers.

PREPARATION TIME: 10 MINUTES +   COOKING TIME: NIL

Herb pancakes with avocado butter

MOULDED EGG AND CAVIAR DIP

7 eggs

3 tablespoons finely chopped flat-leaf (Italian) parsley

60 g (2¼ oz/¼ cup) whole-egg mayonnaise

80 g (2¾ oz/3 bunches) chives, finely snipped

500 g (1 lb 2 oz/2 cups) cream cheese, softened

90 g (3¼ oz) lumpfish roe or caviar

300 g (10½ oz) sour cream

snipped chives and lumpfish roe or caviar to garnish

SERVES 10–12

Fill a saucepan with cold water and gently add the eggs. Bring to the boil, then reduce the heat and simmer for 6 minutes. Drain, then plunge the eggs in cold water to stop the cooking process. Cool thoroughly and drain. Peel the eggs and mash well, then stir in the parsley and mayonnaise. Season to taste.

Line a deep 18 cm (7 inch) loose-based, fluted flan (tart) tin with plastic wrap, leaving a wide overhang to help you remove the moulded dip from the tin later.

Spoon half the egg mixture into the tin. Firmly press down and smooth the surface with a spatula or the back of a spoon, pressing well into the side of the tin. Sprinkle with half the chives, pressing them down into the dip. Using a clean, warm spatula, spread half the cream cheese over the top. Spoon half the roe over the top and gently press down.

Repeat the layering with the remaining egg mixture, chives, cream cheese and roe. Cover the moulded dip with plastic wrap, pressing down firmly so the layers stick together, and refrigerate for 2 hours.

Remove the top cover of plastic wrap and place a plate over the mould. Flip over onto the plate while holding the tin, and then gently ease the tin off. Remove the plastic wrap, trying not to damage the fluted edges.

Spoon dollops of the sour cream over the top of the mould and spread out a little. Decorate with the extra chives and roe. Serve with water crackers.

PREPARATION TIME: 1 HOUR +   COOKING TIME: 6 MINUTES

FRESH OYSTERS WITH TARRAGON VINAIGRETTE

1 tablespoon chopped tarragon
2 teaspoons very finely chopped spring onion (scallion)
2 teaspoons white wine vinegar
1 tablespoon lemon juice
2 tablespoons extra virgin olive oil
24 fresh oysters, on the shell

SERVES 4

To make the vinaigrette, whisk together the tarragon, spring onion, vinegar, lemon juice and olive oil in a bowl.

Remove the oysters from their shells, keeping the shells. Mix the oysters with the vinaigrette, cover and chill for 30 minutes. Rinse and refrigerate the oyster shells as well.

To serve, spoon the oysters back into their shells. Drizzle with any remaining vinaigrette.

PREPARATION TIME: 15 MINUTES +   COOKING TIME: NIL

GRAVLAX WITH MUSTARD SAUCE

55 g (2 oz/¼ cup) sugar
2 tablespoons sea salt
1 teaspoon crushed black peppercorns
2.5 kg (5 lb 8 oz) salmon, filleted, skin on
1 tablespoon vodka or brandy
4 tablespoons very finely chopped dill

MUSTARD SAUCE
1½ tablespoons cider vinegar
1 teaspoon caster (superfine) sugar
125 ml (4 fl oz/½ cup) olive oil
2 teaspoons chopped dill
2 tablespoons dijon mustard

SERVES 12

Combine the sugar, salt and peppercorns in a small dish. Remove any bones from the salmon with tweezers. Pat dry with paper towels and lay a fillet, skin side down, in a shallow tray or ovenproof dish. Sprinkle the fillet with half the vodka, rub half the sugar mixture into the flesh, then sprinkle with half the dill. Sprinkle the remaining vodka over the second salmon fillet and rub the remaining sugar mixture into the flesh. Lay it, flesh side down, on top of the other fillet. Cover with plastic wrap, place a heavy board on top and then weigh the board down with three heavy tins or a foil-covered brick. Refrigerate for 24 hours, turning it over after 12 hours.

To make the mustard sauce, whisk all the ingredients together, then cover until needed.

Uncover the salmon and lay the fillets on a wooden board. Brush off the dill and seasoning with a stiff pastry brush. Sprinkle with the remaining dill, pressing it onto the salmon flesh, shaking off any excess. Serve whole on the serving board, or thinly sliced on an angle towards the tail, with the sauce.

PREPARATION TIME: 10 MINUTES +   COOKING TIME: NIL

NOTE: Gravlax can be refrigerated, covered, for up to a week.

Fresh oysters with tarragon vinaigrette

SEAFOOD QUENELLES

QUENELLES
200 g (7 oz) skinless firm white fish fillets
150 g (5½ oz) scallops
150 g (5½ oz) raw prawn (shrimp) meat
1 egg white
1 teaspoon finely grated lemon zest
125 ml (4 fl oz/½ cup) pouring
(whipping) cream
3 tablespoons finely snipped chives
1 litre (35 fl oz/4 cups) fish stock

TOMATO COULIS
1 tablespoon olive oil
1 garlic clove, crushed
425 g (15 oz) tinned crushed tomatoes
170 ml (5½ fl oz/⅔ cup) fish stock
or water
2 tablespoons pouring (whipping) cream
2 tablespoons snipped chives

SERVES 4

To make the quenelles, pat the fish, scallops and prawn meat dry with paper towels. Roughly mince the fish in a food processor for 30 seconds, then remove. Process the scallops and prawn meat, then return the fish to the processor, add the egg white and lemon zest, and process for about 30 seconds, or until finely minced.

With the motor running, slowly pour in the cream until the mixture just thickens — do not overprocess. Stir in the chives, then transfer to a bowl. Cover and refrigerate for at least 3 hours.

Using two wet tablespoons, mould 2 tablespoons of mixture at a time into egg shapes. Place on a baking tray lined with baking paper. Cover and refrigerate for 30 minutes.

To make the tomato coulis, heat the oil in a saucepan, add the garlic and stir over medium heat for 30 seconds. Add the tomatoes, stock or water, and season. Simmer for 30 minutes, stirring occasionally, until thickened and reduced.

Push the tomato mixture through a fine sieve, discard the pulp and return the liquid to the cleaned pan. Add the cream and chives and reheat gently, stirring occasionally.

In a large frying pan, heat the fish stock until just simmering, but be careful not to boil the stock. Gently lower the quenelles into the poaching liquid in batches, then cover the pan, reduce the heat and poach each batch for about 5-6 minutes, or until cooked through. Lift out using a slotted spoon and drain on crumpled paper towels.

Spoon some of the tomato coulis onto each serving plate and top with the seafood quenelles.

PREPARATION TIME: 30 MINUTES +   COOKING TIME: 40 MINUTES

CRUNCHY PRAWN COCKTAILS

50 g (1³/4 oz) dried rice vermicelli
oil, for deep-frying
sea salt, for sprinkling
750 g (1 lb 10 oz) cooked prawns (shrimp)
1 small iceberg lettuce, leaves separated
1 Lebanese (short) cucumber, sliced
1 avocado, sliced
125 g (4¹/2 oz/¹/2 cup) whole-egg
mayonnaise
1 tablespoon tomato sauce (ketchup)
a few drops Tabasco sauce
lime wedges, to serve

SERVES 6

Break the vermicelli into smaller pieces. Fill a deep-fryer or large heavy-based saucepan one-third full of oil and heat to 180°C (350°F), or until a cube of bread dropped into the oil browns in 15 seconds. Add the noodles to the oil in batches and cook for 10 seconds or until puffed, white and crisp. Drain on crumpled paper towels and sprinkle with sea salt.

Peel the prawns, leaving the tail intact. Gently pull out the dark vein from each prawn back, starting from the head end. Arrange the lettuce and crispy noodles in six shallow bowls and top with the cucumber, avocado and prawns.

Put the mayonnaise, tomato sauce, Tabasco sauce and 1 tablespoon water in a small bowl and whisk to combine. Drizzle the sauce over the prawns and serve with lime wedges.

PREPARATION TIME: 20 MINUTES   COOKING TIME: 5 MINUTES

PORT AND PEPPER PÂTÉ WITH MOON TOASTS

450 g (1 lb) chicken livers
100 g (3¹/2 oz) butter
1 onion, chopped
2 garlic cloves, crushed
80 ml (2¹/2 fl oz/¹/3 cup) port
80 ml (2¹/2 fl oz/¹/3 cup) pouring
(whipping) cream
1 tablespoon snipped chives
60 g (2¹/4 oz) bottled green peppercorns,
drained and lightly crushed
10 slices bread
lemon pepper, to season

MAKES ABOUT 30

Discard any green or discoloured parts from the livers, then chop them. Heat the butter in a large, heavy-based frying pan. Add the liver, onion, garlic and port and stir over medium heat until the liver is almost cooked and the onion is soft. Bring to the boil and simmer for 5 minutes.

Remove from the heat and cool slightly. Combine in a food processor in short bursts until smooth. Press through a fine sieve into a bowl, then stir in the cream, chives and peppercorns. Spoon into a large dish, cover and refrigerate overnight, or until firm.

Preheat the oven to 180°C (350°F/Gas 4). Line a baking tray with foil. To make the toasts, cut shapes out of the bread using a moon-shaped cutter. Place on the tray and sprinkle with the lemon pepper. Bake for 5 minutes, or until pale golden and crisp. Cool on a wire rack. Serve with the pâté.

PREPARATION TIME: 40 MINUTES +   COOKING TIME: 10 MINUTES

Crunchy prawn cocktails

SCALLOPS ON ASIAN RISOTTO CAKES WITH PESTO

500 ml (17 fl oz/2 cups) vegetable stock

2 tablespoons mirin

1 lemon grass stem, white part only, bruised

2 makrut (kaffir lime) leaves

3 coriander (cilantro) roots

2 tablespoons fish sauce

20 g (3/4 oz) butter

2-3 tablespoons peanut oil

3 red Asian shallots, thinly sliced

4 spring onions (scallions), chopped

3 garlic cloves, chopped

2 tablespoons finely chopped fresh ginger

1 1/4 teaspoons white pepper

140 g (5 oz/2/3 cup) risotto rice

2 tablespoons toasted unsalted chopped peanuts

50 g (1 3/4 oz) chopped coriander (cilantro) leaves

2 garlic cloves, extra, chopped

1 teaspoon finely chopped fresh ginger, extra

60 ml (2 fl oz/1/4 cup) lime juice

1-2 teaspoons grated palm sugar (jaggery) or soft brown sugar

vegetable oil, for pan-frying

plain (all-purpose) flour, to dust

1 tablespoon vegetable oil, extra

16 large white scallops without roe

lime slices, to serve

coriander (cilantro) leaves, extra, to garnish

SERVES 4

Heat the stock, mirin, lemon grass, makrut (kaffir lime) leaves, coriander roots, half the fish sauce and 250 ml (9 fl oz/1 cup) water in a saucepan, bring to the boil, then reduce the heat and keep at a simmer.

Heat the butter and 1 tablespoon of the peanut oil in a large saucepan over medium heat until bubbling. Add the shallot, spring onion, garlic, ginger and 1 teaspoon of the white pepper and cook for 2-3 minutes, or until fragrant and the onion is soft. Add the rice and stir until coated.

Add 125 ml (4 fl oz/1/2 cup) of the stock (avoid the lemon grass and coriander roots). Stir constantly over medium heat until nearly all the liquid is absorbed. Continue adding the stock 125 ml (4 fl oz/1/2 cup) at a time, stirring constantly, for 20-25 minutes, or until all the stock is absorbed and the rice is tender and creamy. Remove from the heat, cool, then cover and refrigerate for 3 hours, or until cold.

To make the pesto, combine the peanuts, coriander leaves, extra garlic and ginger and the remaining pepper in a blender or food processor and process until finely chopped. With the motor running, slowly add the lime juice, sugar and remaining fish sauce and peanut oil and process until smooth — you might not need all the oil.

Divide the risotto into four balls, then mould into patties. Cover and refrigerate for 10 minutes. Heat the vegetable oil in a large frying pan over medium heat. Dust the patties with flour and cook in batches for 2 minutes each side, or until crisp. Drain on paper towels. Cover and keep warm.

Heat the extra vegetable oil in a clean frying pan over high heat. Cook the scallops in batches for 1 minute each side. Serve a cake with four scallops, some pesto and lime slices. Garnish with the extra coriander leaves.

PREPARATION TIME: 35 MINUTES +   COOKING TIME: 40 MINUTES

HERBED POTATOES

12 small boiling potatoes
30 g (1 oz) butter
1 tablespoon snipped chives
1 tablespoon lemon thyme
sea salt

Cook the potatoes in a saucepan of boiling water for about 10 minutes, or until just tender. Add the butter, chives and lemon thyme.

Cover with a lid and shake over low heat until the butter has melted. Season to taste with sea salt.

SERVES 4   PREPARATION TIME: 5 MINUTES   COOKING TIME: 10 MINUTES

CELERIAC AND TARRAGON PURÉE

500 ml (17 fl oz/2 cups) vegetable stock
60 ml (2 fl oz/¹/₄ cup) lemon juice
3 celeriacs, peeled and chopped
40 g (1¹/₂ oz) butter
1 tablespoon pouring (whipping) cream
1 tablespoon finely chopped tarragon

SERVES 6

Pour the vegetable stock, lemon juice and 500 ml (17 fl oz/2 cups) water into a saucepan and bring to the boil. Add the celeriac and cook for 10–15 minutes, or until tender. You may need to add extra water, depending on the size of the celeriac.

Drain and place in a food processor with the butter and cream. Season and process until smooth. Alternatively, mash until smooth. Stir in the chopped tarragon. If the mixture is too thick, add a little more cream.

PREPARATION TIME: 15 MINUTES   COOKING TIME: 15 MINUTES

Herbed potatoes

FRISÉE AND GARLIC CROUTON SALAD

VINAIGRETTE
1 French shallot, finely chopped
1 tablespoon dijon mustard
60 ml (2 fl oz/¼ cup) tarragon vinegar
170 ml (5½ fl oz/⅔ cup) extra virgin
olive oil

1 tablespoon olive oil
250 g (9 oz) speck, rind removed, cut into
5 mm x 2 cm (¼ x ¾ inch) pieces
½ baguette, sliced
4 garlic cloves
1 baby frisée (curly endive)
100 g (3½ oz) walnuts, toasted

SERVES 4–6

To make the vinaigrette, whisk together the shallot, mustard and vinegar in a small bowl. Slowly add the oil, whisking constantly until thickened. Set aside.

Heat the oil in a large frying pan, add the speck, bread and garlic and cook over medium–high heat for 5–8 minutes, or until the bread and speck are both crisp. Remove the garlic from the pan.

Put the frisée, baguette, speck, walnuts and vinaigrette in a large bowl. Toss together well and serve.

PREPARATION TIME: 20 MINUTES   COOKING TIME: 10 MINUTES

WATERCRESS SALAD

500 g (1 lb 2 oz) watercress
3 celery stalks
1 cucumber
3 oranges
1 red onion, thinly sliced into rings
35 g (1¼ oz) snipped chives
60 g (2¼ oz/½ cup) chopped pecans or
walnuts

DRESSING
60 ml (2 fl oz/¼ cup) olive oil
60 ml (2 fl oz/¼ cup) lemon juice
2 teaspoons grated orange zest
1 teaspoon wholegrain mustard
1 tablespoon honey

SERVES 4–6

Break the watercress into small sprigs, discarding the coarser stems. Cut the celery into thin 5 cm (2 inch) long sticks. Peel, halve and seed the cucumber and cut into thin slices. Peel the oranges, remove all the white pith and cut the oranges into segments between the membrane. Refrigerate until needed.

To make the dressing, whisk together the oil, lemon juice, orange zest, mustard, honey and some freshly ground black pepper.

Combine all the salad ingredients except the nuts in a serving bowl. Pour the dressing over and toss. Sprinkle with the pecans or walnuts.

PREPARATION TIME: 35 MINUTES   COOKING TIME: NIL

PROSCIUTTO, CAMEMBERT AND FIG SALAD

60 g (2¼ oz) thinly sliced prosciutto
1 curly oak leaf lettuce
4 fresh figs, quartered
100 g (3½ oz) camembert cheese,
thinly sliced
1 garlic clove, crushed
1 tablespoon mustard
2 tablespoons white wine vinegar
80 ml (2½ fl oz/⅓ cup) olive oil

SERVES 4

Grill (broil) the prosciutto until crisp.

Arrange the lettuce leaves on a large plate and top with the figs, camembert and prosciutto.

Whisk together the garlic, mustard, vinegar and olive oil and drizzle over the salad.

PREPARATION TIME: 10 MINUTES   COOKING TIME: 5 MINUTES

Watercress salad

STUFFED ARTICHOKES

125 ml (4 fl oz/¹/₂ cup) lemon juice
12 globe artichokes
500 g (1 lb 2 oz) minced (ground) lamb
40 g (1¹/₂ oz/¹/₂ cup) fresh breadcrumbs
1 egg, lightly beaten
1 tablespoon chopped thyme
olive oil, for deep-frying
125 ml (4 fl oz/¹/₂ cup) extra virgin olive oil
¹/₂ teaspoon ground turmeric
1 bay leaf
375 ml (13 fl oz/1¹/₂ cups) chicken stock
40 g (1¹/₂ oz) butter
2 tablespoons plain (all-purpose) flour

SERVES 6

Fill a large bowl with water and add 60 ml (2 fl oz/¹/₄ cup) of the lemon juice. Peel the outer leaves from the artichokes, trimming the bases and stems to reveal the bases. Cut the tops off to reveal the chokes and remove the chokes. Put the artichokes in the bowl of acidulated water.

Put the lamb, breadcrumbs, egg and thyme in a bowl, season and mix well. Pat the artichokes dry with paper towels and fill each with 2 tablespoons of the lamb mixture.

Fill a deep-fryer or large heavy-based saucepan one-third full of olive oil and heat to 180°C (350°F), or until a cube of bread dropped into the oil browns in 15 seconds. Cook the artichokes in batches for 5 minutes, or until golden brown. Drain well.

Put the extra virgin olive oil, turmeric, bay leaf, remaining lemon juice and 250 ml (9 fl oz/1 cup) of the stock in a 1.25 litre (44 fl oz/5-cup) flameproof casserole dish. Season, then bring to the boil. Add the artichokes, reduce the heat, cover and simmer for 1 hour, or until tender, adding more stock if necessary. Turn the artichokes twice during cooking. Remove the artichokes and keep them warm. Reserve the cooking liquid.

Melt the butter in a saucepan, add the flour and stir for 1 minute, or until pale and foamy. Remove from the heat and gradually stir in the reserved cooking liquid. Return to the heat and stir until the sauce boils and thickens, then reduce the heat and simmer for 2 minutes. Serve immediately with the artichokes.

PREPARATION TIME: 1 HOUR 30 MINUTES COOKING TIME: 1 HOUR 25 MINUTES

ASPARAGUS WITH CITRUS HOLLANDAISE

24 asparagus spears, woody ends trimmed
185 g (6¹/₂ oz) butter
4 egg yolks
1–2 tablespoons lemon, lime or orange juice
shavings of parmesan or pecorino cheese (optional)

SERVES 4

Put the asparagus in a saucepan of boiling water. Simmer for 2–4 minutes, or until just tender. Drain well.

Melt the butter in a small saucepan. Skim any froth from the top and discard. Allow the butter to cool.

Combine the egg yolks and 2 tablespoons water in a small saucepan and whisk for 30 seconds, or until pale and creamy. Place the pan over very low heat and continue whisking for 3 minutes, or until the mixture thickens.

Remove from the heat. Add the cooled butter gradually, whisking constantly (leave the whey in the bottom of the pan). Stir in the lemon, lime or orange juice and season to taste. Drizzle the sauce over the asparagus and garnish with cheese shavings (if desired).

PREPARATION TIME: 15 MINUTES   COOKING TIME: 8 MINUTES

GOLDEN MUSHROOM TART

1 sheet frozen puff pastry, thawed
2 tablespoons oil
2 onions, thinly sliced
1 tablespoon red wine vinegar
60 g (2¹/₄ oz) butter
350 g (12 oz) assorted mushrooms
marjoram, to sprinkle
25 g (1 oz/¹/₄ cup) freshly grated parmesan cheese

SERVES 4

Preheat the oven to 200°C (400°F/Gas 6). Place the puff pastry on a non-stick baking tray. Heat the oil in a frying pan, then add the onion and vinegar. Cook over low heat for 20–30 minutes, or until golden brown and caramelized. Remove from the pan, then cool slightly on paper towels.

Add the butter and mushrooms to the pan and cook for 5 minutes, or until tender. Drain off any excess liquid and cool on paper towels. Season to taste.

Cook the puff pastry for 10 minutes, then very carefully and quickly spread the onion over the puff pastry base, leaving a 2 cm (³/₄ inch) border. Top with the mushrooms and sprinkle with marjoram and grated parmesan. Cook for another 10 minutes, or until golden.

PREPARATION TIME: 10 MINUTES   COOKING TIME: 35 MINUTES

Asparagus with citrus hollandaise

CRISPY FRIED CRAB

1 kg (2 lb 4 oz) fresh mud crab
1 egg, lightly beaten
1 red chilli, finely chopped
1/2 teaspoon crushed garlic
1/4 teaspoon ground white pepper
oil, for deep-frying
lemon wedges, to serve

SEASONING MIX
40 g (1 1/2 oz/ 1/3 cup) plain
(all-purpose) flour
60 g (2 1/4 oz/ 1/3 cup) rice flour
3 teaspoons caster (superfine) sugar
1 teaspoon ground white pepper

SERVES 4

Freeze the crab for about 1 hour until immobilized. Scrub the crab clean. Pull back the apron and remove the top shell (it should come off easily and in one piece). Remove the intestines and the grey feathery gills. Twist off the legs and claws. Using a sharp, heavy knife, chop the body into four pieces. Crack the claws with a good hit with the back of a knife.

Beat the egg with the chilli, garlic, pepper and 1/2 teaspoon salt in a large bowl. Put the crab pieces in the mixture, cover and refrigerate for 1 hour.

Sift the seasoning ingredients together onto a large plate. Dip all the crab segments in the seasoning and dust off any excess.

Fill a deep-fryer or heavy-based saucepan one-third full of oil and heat to 180°C (350°F), or until a cube of bread dropped into the oil browns in 15 seconds. Carefully cook the claws in batches for 7–8 minutes, the body portions for 3–4 minutes, and the legs for 2 minutes. Drain on crumpled paper towels before serving with lemon wedges.

PREPARATION TIME: 30 MINUTES +   COOKING TIME: 15 MINUTES

NOTE: Serve the the crab as soon as it's cooked. You will need a crab cracker to crack the claws so you can remove the flesh.

TAGLIATELLE WITH CHICKEN LIVERS AND CREAM

375 g (13 oz) tagliatelle
300 g (10½ oz) chicken livers
2 tablespoons olive oil
1 onion, finely chopped
1 garlic clove, crushed
250 ml (9 fl oz/1 cup) pouring (whipping) cream
1 tablespoon snipped chives
1 teaspoon wholegrain mustard
2 eggs, beaten
freshly grated parmesan cheese, to serve
snipped chives, to serve

SERVES 4

Cook the tagliatelle in a large saucepan of rapidly boiling salted water until *al dente*. Drain and return to the pan.

While the pasta is cooking, trim any green or discoloured parts from the chicken livers, then slice them. Heat the olive oil in a large frying pan. Add the onion and garlic and stir over low heat until the onion is tender.

Add the chicken liver to the pan and cook gently for 2–3 minutes. Remove from the heat and stir in the cream, chives and mustard and season to taste. Return to the heat and bring to the boil. Add the beaten eggs and stir quickly to combine. Remove from the heat.

Add the sauce to the hot pasta and toss well to combine. Serve sprinkled with parmesan and snipped chives.

PREPARATION TIME: 20 MINUTES   COOKING TIME: 15 MINUTES

CARAMELIZED ONION AND BLUE CHEESE RISONI

30 g (1 oz) butter
60 ml (2 fl oz/¼ cup) olive oil
4 onions, sliced
500 g (1 lb 2 oz) risoni
185 g (6½ oz) blue cheese
100 g (3½ oz) mascarpone cheese
130 g (4½ oz/2 cups) shredded English spinach

SERVES 4

Heat the butter and the olive oil in a large heavy-based frying pan. Add the onion and cook over low heat for 20–30 minutes, or until golden brown and caramelized. Remove from the pan with a slotted spoon and drain on paper towels.

Meanwhile, cook the risoni in a saucepan of rapidly boiling salted water until *al dente*. Drain well and return to the pan.

Mix the blue cheese, mascarpone and onion in a bowl. Add to the cooked risoni with the spinach and toss through. Season to taste before serving.

PREPARATION TIME: 20 MINUTES   COOKING TIME: 35 MINUTES

Tagliatelle with chicken livers and cream

RACK OF LAMB WITH HERB CRUST

2 x 6-rib racks of lamb, French-trimmed
1 tablespoon oil
80 g (2³/4 oz/1 cup) fresh breadcrumbs
3 garlic cloves
3 tablespoons finely chopped flat-leaf
(Italian) parsley
2 teapoons thyme leaves
1/2 teaspoon finely grated lemon zest
60 g (2¹/4 oz) butter, softened
250 ml (9 fl oz/1 cup) beef stock
1 garlic clove, extra, finely chopped
1 thyme sprig

SERVES 4

Preheat the oven to 250°C (500°F/Gas 9). Score the fat on the lamb racks in a diamond pattern. Rub with a little oil and season.

Heat the oil in a frying pan over high heat, add the lamb racks and brown for 4-5 minutes. Remove and set aside. Do not wash the pan as you will need it later.

In a large bowl, mix the breadcrumbs, garlic, parsley, thyme leaves and lemon zest. Season, then mix in the butter to form a paste.

Firmly press a layer of breadcrumb mixture over the fat on the lamb racks, leaving the bones and base clean. Bake in a roasting tin for 12 minutes for medium-rare. Rest the lamb on a plate while you make the jus.

To make the jus, add the beef stock, extra garlic and thyme sprig to the roasting tin juices, scraping the pan. Return this liquid to the original frying pan and simmer over high heat for 5-8 minutes, or until the sauce has reduced. Strain and serve with the lamb.

PREPARATION TIME: 25 MINUTES   COOKING TIME: 25 MINUTES

RABBIT CASSEROLE WITH MUSTARD SAUCE

2 rabbits (800 g/1 lb 12 oz each)
2 tablespoons olive oil
2 onions, sliced
4 bacon slices, cut into 3 cm (1¼ inch) pieces
2 tablespoons plain (all-purpose) flour
375 ml (13 fl oz/1½ cups) chicken stock
125 ml (4 fl oz/½ cup) dry white wine
1 teaspoon thyme leaves
125 ml (4 fl oz/½ cup) pouring (whipping) cream
2 tablespoons dijon mustard
thyme sprigs, to garnish

SERVES 4–6

Preheat the oven to 180°C (350°F/Gas 4). Wash the rabbits under cold water and pat dry with paper towels. Cut along both sides of the backbones with kitchen scissors and discard. Cut each rabbit into eight even-sized pieces, remove any fat and pat dry again.

Heat half the oil in a 2.5 litre (88 fl oz/10-cup) flameproof casserole dish. Brown the rabbit in batches, adding oil when necessary, then remove from the dish.

Add the onion and bacon to the casserole dish and cook, stirring, for 5 minutes, or until lightly browned. Sprinkle the flour into the dish and mix. Stir with a wooden spoon to scrape the sediment from the base. Add the stock and wine, and stir until the sauce comes to the boil. Return the rabbit to the casserole dish and add the thyme leaves.

Cover and bake for 1¼–1½ hours, or until the rabbit is tender and the sauce has thickened. Stir in the combined cream and mustard. Garnish with thyme sprigs. Delicious with steamed vegetables.

PREPARATION TIME: 30 MINUTES   COOKING TIME: 2 HOURS

FISH COOKED IN PAPER

4 skinless firm white fish fillets (200 g/7 oz each)
1 leek, white part only, cut into thin batons
4 spring onions (scallions), shredded
30 g (1 oz) butter, softened
1 lemon, cut into 12 very thin slices
2–3 tablespoons lemon juice

SERVES 4

Preheat the oven to 180°C (350°F/Gas 4). Place each fish fillet in the centre of a piece of baking paper large enough to enclose the fish. Season lightly.

Scatter the leek and spring onion over the fish. Top each with a teaspoon of butter and three slices of lemon. Sprinkle with the lemon juice. Bring the paper together and fold over several times. Fold the ends under. Bake on a baking tray for 20 minutes (the steam will make the paper puff up), or until the fish flakes easily when tested with a fork. Serve as parcels or lift the fish out and pour the juices over the top before serving.

PREPARATION TIME: 20 MINUTES   COOKING TIME: 20 MINUTES

Rabbit casserole with mustard sauce

SURF 'N' TURF

LEMON MUSTARD SAUCE
30 g (1 oz) butter
1 spring onion (scallion), finely chopped
1 garlic clove, crushed
1 tablespoon plain (all-purpose) flour
250 ml (9 fl oz/1 cup) milk
2 tablespoons pouring (whipping) cream
1 tablespoon lemon juice
2 teaspoons dijon mustard

1 large or 2 small raw lobster tails
2 tablespoons oil
4 beef eye fillets (200 g/7 oz each)
175 g (6 oz) fresh or frozen crabmeat
flat-leaf (Italian) parsley, to garnish

SERVES 4

To make the sauce, melt the butter in a saucepan, add the spring onion and garlic and stir over medium heat for 1 minute, or until the onion has softened. Stir in the flour and cook for 1 minute, or until pale and foaming. Remove from the heat and gradually stir in the milk. Return to the heat and stir constantly until the sauce boils and thickens. Reduce the heat and simmer for 2 minutes. Remove from the heat and stir in the cream, lemon juice and mustard. Keep warm.

Starting at the end where the head was, cut down each side of the lobster shell on the underside with kitchen scissors. Pull back the flap and remove the meat from the shell. Heat half the oil in a frying pan, add the lobster meat and cook over medium heat for 3 minutes each side (longer if using a large tail), or until just cooked through. Remove from the pan and keep warm. Reserve the oil in the pan.

Meanwhile, heat the remaining oil in a separate frying pan, add the steaks and cook over high heat for 2 minutes each side to seal, turning once. For rare steaks, cook each side 1 more minute. For medium and well-done steaks, reduce the heat to medium and continue cooking for 2–3 minutes each side for medium or 4–6 minutes each side for well done. Remove from the pan and keep warm.

Add the crab to the reserved lobster pan and stir until heated through. To serve, place the steaks on plates. Top with crab followed by slices of lobster. Pour the sauce over the top and garnish with parsley.

PREPARATION TIME: 20 MINUTES   COOKING TIME: 15–20 MINUTES

POACHED SALMON WITH DILL MAYONNAISE

2 litres (70 fl oz/8 cups) dry white wine
60 ml (2 fl oz/¼ cup) white wine vinegar
2 onions
10 whole cloves
4 carrots, chopped
1 lemon, quartered
2 bay leaves
1 teaspoon black peppercorns
4 sprigs flat-leaf (Italian) parsley
2.5 kg (5 lb 8 oz) Atlantic salmon, cleaned gutted and scaled
watercress and lemon slices, to garnish

DILL MAYONNAISE
1 egg, at room temperature
1 egg yolk, extra, at room temperature,
1 tablespoon lemon juice
1 teaspoon white wine vinegar
375 ml (13 fl oz/1½ cups) light olive oil
1 tablespoon chopped dill

SERVES 8–10

Put the wine, vinegar and 2.5 litres (88 fl oz/10 cups) water in a large heavy-based saucepan. Stud the onions with the cloves. Add to the pan with the carrot, lemon, bay leaves, peppercorns and parsley. Bring to the boil, reduce the heat and simmer for 30–35 minutes. Cool. Strain into a fish kettle (poacher) that will hold the salmon. Put the whole fish in the fish kettle and cover. Bring to the boil, reduce the heat and poach gently for 10–15 minutes, or until the fish flakes when tested in the thickest part with a fork. Remove from the heat and cool the fish in the liquid.

To make the mayonnaise, process the egg, extra yolk, lemon juice and vinegar in a food processor or blender for 10 seconds, or until blended. With the motor running, add the oil in a thin, steady stream, blending until all the oil is added and the mayonnaise is thick and creamy. Transfer to a bowl, stir in the dill, and season to taste.

Remove the fish from the liquid, place on a work surface or serving platter and peel back the skin. Garnish with trimmed watercress and lemon slices and serve with the dill mayonnaise.

PREPARATION TIME: 40 MINUTES   COOKING TIME: 1 HOUR

CARPETBAG STEAK

4 rib-eye steaks (4 cm/1½ inches thick)
8 fresh oysters, shelled
1 teaspoon chopped flat-leaf (Italian) parsley
2 teaspoons lemon juice
2 tablespoons oil
250 ml (9 fl oz/1 cup) beef stock
2 teaspoons worcestershire sauce
60 g (2¼ oz) butter, chopped
thyme, to garnish

SERVES 4

Trim the meat of excess fat and sinew. Cut a deep pocket in the side of each steak. Combine the oysters, parsley, lemon juice and some pepper in a bowl. Spoon evenly into the pockets and secure with toothpicks. Heat the oil in a heavy-based frying pan, add the steaks and cook over high heat for 2 minutes each side to seal. For rare steaks, cook for another minute each side. Reduce the heat to medium–high and cook for another 2–3 minutes each side for medium or 4–6 minutes each side for well done. Remove and drain on crumpled paper towels. Cover and keep warm.

Bring the stock and sauce to the boil in a saucepan. Reduce the heat, stir in the butter until melted, then pour over the steaks. Garnish with thyme.

PREPARATION TIME: 15 MINUTES   COOKING TIME: 15 MINUTES

Poached salmon with dill mayonnaise

VEAL WRAPPED IN PROSCIUTTO WITH HONEYED WILD RICE

500 g (1 lb 2 oz/1 bunch) English spinach, stalks removed

4 veal steaks (200 g/7 oz each), slightly flattened

2 tablespoons wholegrain mustard

16 slices prosciutto

2 tablespoons olive oil

2 garlic cloves, crushed

125 ml (4 fl oz/½ cup) dry white wine

250 ml (9 fl oz/1 cup) chicken stock

1 tablespoon dijon mustard

1 teaspoon cornflour (cornstarch), blended with 2 tablespoons cold water

1 tablespoon chervil sprigs

HONEYED WILD RICE

210 g (7½ oz/1 cup) wild rice blend

30 g (1 oz) butter

1 onion, finely chopped

1 garlic clove, crushed

1 tablespoon honey

1 tablespoon light soy sauce

SERVES 4

Preheat the oven to 180°C (350°F/Gas 4). Steam the spinach until just wilted, then rinse in cold water, drain and pat dry. Put a few spinach leaves on a board to form a square, a little larger than the veal steak. Also on the board, lay out four prosciutto slices, slightly overlapping, with the short ends towards you. Put the steak on the spinach square, spread it with wholegrain mustard and roll up both the veal and spinach to form a log. Lay the veal and spinach log across the bottom edge of the pieces of prosciutto and roll up, folding in the sides as you go to form a parcel. Repeat with the remaining spinach, veal and prosciutto until you end up with four parcels.

To make the honeyed wild rice, bring a large saucepan of water to the boil. Add the rice and cook, stirring occasionally, for 25 minutes, or until tender, then drain. Heat the butter in a small frying pan, add the onion and garlic and cook until the onion is softened but not browned. Add the rice, honey and soy sauce, toss thoroughly, then remove from the heat.

Meanwhile, heat the oil in a frying pan over medium heat and cook the veal parcels until lightly browned, turning frequently. Remove from the pan and transfer to a roasting tin. Bake for 10–15 minutes. Remove from the oven, cover and keep warm.

Put the roasting tin on the stove-top over medium heat, add the garlic and wine and cook for 2 minutes. Add the stock, dijon mustard and cornflour paste. Stir until the sauce boils and thickens. Strain. Slice the veal thickly, pour over the sauce and sprinkle with chervil.

PREPARATION TIME: 25 MINUTES   COOKING TIME: 35 MINUTES

JOHN DORY WITH PRAWNS AND CREAMY DILL SAUCE

12 raw large prawns (shrimp)
625 ml (21^1/$_2$ fl oz/2^1/$_2$ cups) fish stock
30 g (1 oz) butter
1 garlic clove, finely chopped
2 tablespoons plain (all-purpose) flour
2 tablespoons pouring (whipping) cream
oil, for pan-frying
4 john dory fillets (200 g/7 oz each)
1 tablespoon snipped chives
1 tablespoon chopped dill
chives or dill sprigs, to garnish

SERVES 4

Peel the prawns, leaving the tails intact. Gently pull out the dark vein from each prawn back, starting from the head end. Heat the stock in a saucepan and bring to the boil. Reduce the heat and simmer for 10 minutes, or until the liquid has reduced. You will need 375 ml (13 fl oz/1^1/$_2$ cups) fish stock.

Melt the butter in a small saucepan and add the garlic. Stir in the flour and cook for 1 minute, or until pale and foaming. Remove from the heat and gradually stir in the stock. Return to the heat and stir constantly until the sauce boils and thickens. Reduce the heat and simmer for 1 minute. Remove from the heat and stir in the cream. Season to taste. Keep warm.

Heat a little oil in a frying pan and cook the fish fillets over medium heat for 2 minutes each side, or until the fish flakes easily when tested with a fork. Transfer to serving plates. Add the prawns to the same pan (add more oil to the pan if necessary) and cook for 2–3 minutes. Stir the chives and dill into the sauce, arrange the prawns on top of the fish and spoon the sauce over the top. Garnish with chives or dill.

PREPARATION TIME: 15 MINUTES   COOKING TIME: 20 MINUTES

TUNA WITH SORREL HOLLANDAISE

4 tuna steaks (150 g/5^1/$_2$ oz each)
2 tablespoons olive oil

SORREL HOLLANDAISE
15 young sorrel leaves, stems removed
150 g (5^1/$_2$ oz) butter
3 egg yolks
1 tablespoon lemon juice

SERVES 4

Brush the tuna with the oil. Heat a large frying pan and cook the tuna for 2–3 minutes each side over medium heat. Remove from the pan, cover and keep warm.

To make the sorrel hollandaise, put the sorrel leaves in a bowl, cover with boiling water, drain and rinse in cold water. Pat the leaves dry with paper towels and chop roughly. Melt the butter in a small saucepan. Put the egg yolks in a food processor and process for 20 seconds. With the motor running, add the hot butter in a thin, steady stream and process until thick and creamy. Add the lemon juice and sorrel and season to taste. Process for another 20 seconds. Spoon the sorrel hollandaise over the tuna and serve.

PREPARATION TIME: 15 MINUTES   COOKING TIME: 10 MINUTES

John dory with prawns and creamy dill sauce

SEAFOOD TERRINE

FIRST LAYER

500 g (1 lb 2 oz) raw prawns
(shrimp), chilled
2 egg whites, chilled
pinch freshly grated nutmeg
250 ml (9 fl oz/1 cup) pouring (whipping)
cream, chilled
150 g (5½ oz) baby green beans, trimmed

SECOND LAYER

250 g (9 oz) skinless salmon or ocean
trout fillet, chopped
2 egg whites, chilled
2 tablespoons snipped chives
250 ml (9 fl oz/1 cup) pouring (whipping)
cream, chilled

TOMATO COULIS

750 g (1 lb 10 oz) very ripe roma (plum)
tomatoes
2 tablespoons extra virgin olive oil
1 onion, very finely chopped
2 tablespoons Grand Marnier (optional)
trimmed watercress, to garnish

SERVES 8

Preheat the oven to 180°C (350°F/Gas 4). Brush a 1.5 litre (52 fl oz/6-cup) loaf (bar) tin, measuring 12 x 22 cm (4½ x 8½ inches), with oil and line the base with baking paper.

To make the first layer, peel the prawns and gently pull out the dark vein from each prawn back, starting at the head end. Finely chop the prawns in a food processor. Add the egg whites one at a time, processing until smooth. Season with salt, pepper and nutmeg. Gradually add the cream. Don't overprocess or it may curdle. Spoon into the prepared loaf tin, cover and refrigerate.

Cook the beans in boiling water for 3 minutes, or until just tender, then drain and plunge into cold water. Drain and dry with paper towels. Arrange lengthways over the prawn mixture.

To make the second layer, process the fish in a food processor until finely chopped. Add the egg whites one at a time and process until smooth. Add the chives. Gradually pour in the cream. Do not overprocess or it may curdle. Spread evenly over the beans.

Cover the terrine tightly with foil brushed with oil and put in a baking tray. Pour cold water into the tray to come halfway up the side of the tin. Bake for 35 minutes, or until lightly set in the centre. Cool before removing the foil. Cover with plastic wrap and refrigerate until firm. Serve at room temperature.

Meanwhile, to make the tomato coulis, score a cross in the base of each tomato. Put in a heatproof bowl and cover with boiling water. Leave for 30 seconds, then transfer to cold water, drain and peel away the skin from the cross. Cut the tomatoes in half, scoop out the seeds and chop the flesh. Heat the oil in a saucepan, add the onion and stir for 2–3 minutes, or until tender. Add the tomato and cook over medium heat, stirring often, for 8 minutes, or until reduced and thickened slightly. Stir in the Grand Marnier (if desired) and cook for 1 minute. Cool, then process in a food processor until smooth. Season to taste and serve with slices of terrine, garnished with watercress.

PREPARATION TIME: 1 HOUR +   COOKING TIME: 40 MINUTES

SUMMER CASUALS

ZUCCHINI PATTIES

300 g (10¹/₂ oz) zucchini (courgette), grated
1 small onion, finely chopped
30 g (1 oz/¹/₄ cup) self-raising flour
35 g (1¹/₄ oz/¹/₃ cup) freshly grated kefalotyri or parmesan cheese
1 tablespoon chopped mint
2 teaspoons chopped flat-leaf (Italian) parsley
pinch freshly grated nutmeg
25 g (1 oz/¹/₄ cup) dry breadcrumbs
1 egg, lightly beaten
olive oil, for pan-frying
lemon wedges, to serve

MAKES 16

Put the zucchini and onion in the centre of a clean tea towel (dish towel), gather the corners together and twist as tightly as possible to remove all the juices. Combine the zucchini, onion, flour, cheese, mint, parsley, nutmeg, breadcrumbs and egg in a large bowl. Season well, then mix with your hands to form a stiff mixture that clumps together.

Heat the oil in a large frying pan over medium heat. When hot, drop level tablespoons of mixture into the pan and pan-fry for 2–3 minutes, or until well browned all over. Drain well on crumpled paper towels and serve hot, with lemon wedges.

PREPARATION TIME: 20 MINUTES   COOKING TIME: 15 MINUTES

SCALLOP CEVICHE

16 scallops, on the shell
1 teaspoon finely grated lime zest
2 garlic cloves, chopped
2 red chillies, seeded and chopped
60 ml (2 fl oz/¹/₄ cup) lime juice
1 tablespoon chopped flat-leaf (Italian) parsley
1 tablespoon olive oil

SERVES 2–4

Take the scallops off their shells. Rinse and reserve the shells. If the scallops need to be cut off, use a small, sharp knife to slice them free, being careful to leave as little meat on the shell as possible. Slice or pull off any vein, membrane or hard white muscle, leaving any roe attached.

In a non-metallic bowl, mix together the lime zest, garlic, chilli, lime juice, parsley and olive oil, and season. Put the scallops in the dressing and stir to coat. Cover with plastic wrap and refrigerate for 2 hours to 'cook' the scallop meat.

To serve, slide each scallop back onto a half shell and spoon the dressing over. Serve cold.

PREPARATION TIME: 20 MINUTES +   COOKING TIME: NIL

NOTE: The scallops will keep for 2 days in the dressing.

Zucchini patties

CRAB CAKES WITH AVOCADO SALSA

2 eggs, lightly beaten
340 g (11¾ oz) tinned crabmeat, drained
1 spring onion (scallion), finely chopped
1 tablespoon mayonnaise
2 teaspoons sweet chilli sauce
100 g (3½ oz/1¼ cups) fresh white breadcrumbs
oil, for pan-frying
lime wedges, to serve
coriander (cilantro) leaves, to garnish

AVOCADO SALSA
2 roma (plum) tomatoes, chopped
1 small red onion, finely chopped
1 large avocado, diced
60 ml (2 fl oz/¼ cup) lime juice
2 tablespoons chervil
1 teaspoon caster (superfine) sugar

SERVES 4

Combine the eggs, crabmeat, spring onion, mayonnaise, sweet chilli sauce and breadcrumbs in a bowl. Stir well and season. Using wet hands, form the crab mixture into eight small flat patties. Cover and refrigerate for 30 minutes.

To make the avocado salsa, put the tomato, onion, avocado, lime juice, chervil and sugar in a bowl. Season and toss gently to combine.

Heat the oil in a large heavy-based frying pan to 180°C (350°F), or until a cube of bread dropped into the oil browns in 15 seconds. Cook the crab cakes over medium heat for 6 minutes, or until golden brown on both sides. Drain well on crumpled paper towels. Serve the crab cakes with the bowl of avocado salsa and some lime wedges. Garnish with the coriander leaves.

PREPARATION TIME: 15 MINUTES +   COOKING TIME: 6 MINUTES

WRAPPED PRAWNS WITH MANGO DIP

12 cooked prawns (shrimp)
12 snow peas (mangetout)
lime wedges, to serve

MANGO DIP
125 g (4$\frac{1}{2}$ oz/$\frac{1}{2}$ cup) mayonnaise
2 tablespoons mango chutney
1 teaspoon curry paste
1 tablespoon lime juice

SERVES 4

Peel the prawns, leaving the tails intact. Gently pull out the dark vein from each prawn back, starting from the head end.

Blanch the snow peas and wrap one around each of the prawns. Secure each with a toothpick.

To make the dip, mix together the mayonnaise, mango chutney, curry paste and lime juice. Serve with the snow pea prawns and lime wedges.

PREPARATION TIME: 15 MINUTES   COOKING TIME: NIL

PAN-FRIED HALOUMI WITH LEMON

400 g (14 oz) haloumi cheese
olive oil, for pan-frying
2 tablespoons lemon juice

SERVES 4

Pat the haloumi dry with paper towels and cut into 1 cm ($\frac{1}{2}$ inch) slices.

Pour oil into a large frying pan to 5 mm ($\frac{1}{4}$ inch) depth and heat over medium heat. Add the haloumi and pan-fry for 1 minute each side, or until golden. Remove the pan from the heat and pour the lemon juice over the haloumi. Season with ground black pepper.

Serve straight from the pan or on a serving plate, with crusty bread to mop up the lemon juice and olive oil mixture.

PREPARATION TIME: 5 MINUTES   COOKING TIME: 2 MINUTES

Wrapped prawns with mango dip

EGGPLANT FRITTERS

YOGHURT DIP
200 g (7 oz) plain yoghurt
2 tablespoons finely grated onion
1/2 teaspoon dried mint
1/4 teaspoon ground coriander
pinch ground cumin

1 large, long eggplant (aubergine)
2 tablespoons besan (chickpea flour)
30 g (1 oz/1/4 cup) self-raising flour
55 g (2 oz/1/2 cup) besan (chickpea flour),
extra
2 eggs, lightly beaten
60 ml (2 fl oz/1/4 cup) beer, chilled
2 teaspoons lemon juice
170 ml (5 1/2 fl oz/2/3 cup) olive oil, for
pan-frying

MAKES 20

To make the yoghurt dip, beat all the ingredients with 1/2 teaspoon salt in a small bowl until well combined. Cover the bowl with plastic wrap and refrigerate until needed.

Cut the eggplant into 20 slices, each about 5 mm (1/4 inch) thick. Sprinkle both sides of each slice with salt. Leave in a colander for about 20 minutes. Rinse the eggplant, drain well and pat dry with paper towels.

Combine the 2 tablespoons of besan flour with 1/4 teaspoon black pepper on a sheet of baking paper. Lightly dust the eggplant slices in the seasoned flour and shake off any excess.

Sift the remaining flours into a medium bowl and make a well in the centre. Add the eggs, beer and lemon juice all at once. Beat until all the liquid is incorporated and the batter is free of lumps.

Heat the oil in a large heavy-based frying pan. Using two forks, dip the floured eggplant slices into the batter a few pieces at a time. Drain off the excess. Cook the eggplant in the oil over medium–high heat for 2 minutes, or until the underside is golden and crisp. Turn the fritter over and cook the other side. Transfer to a large plate and keep warm. Repeat with the remaining batter and eggplant. Serve with the chilled yoghurt dip.

PREPARATION TIME: 40 MINUTES +   COOKING TIME: 15–20 MINUTES

SALMON AND FENNEL SALAD

2 fennel bulbs
2 teaspoons dijon mustard
1 teaspoon caster (superfine) sugar
125 ml (4 fl oz/½ cup) olive oil
2 tablespoons lemon juice
200 g (7 oz) smoked salmon, cut into strips
2 tablespoons snipped chives
1 tablespoon chopped dill (optional)
rocket (arugula), to serve

SERVES 4

Trim the fronds from the fennel. Slice the fennel bulbs and chop the fronds.

To make the dressing, whisk together the mustard, sugar, olive oil and lemon juice in a large bowl.

Add the sliced fennel bulb, salmon, chives and 1 tablespoon fennel fronds or dill to the bowl. Season and toss gently. Serve with the rocket and maybe some toast.

PREPARATION TIME: 15 MINUTES   COOKING TIME: NIL

CITRUS AND AVOCADO SALAD

2 avocados, sliced into 1 cm (½ inch) slices
2 oranges, segmented, reserving 1 tablespoon juice
1 grapefruit (preferably pink), segmented
90 g (3¼ oz/2 cups) rocket (arugula)
1 teaspoon finely grated orange zest
80 ml (2½ fl oz/⅓ cup) extra virgin olive oil
1 tablespoon red wine vinegar
½ teaspoon dijon mustard
1 teaspoon sugar
1 tablespoon chopped mint

SERVES 4

Put the avocado, orange and grapefruit in a serving bowl or on a platter and toss gently with the rocket.

Put the orange zest, reserved orange juice, oil, vinegar, mustard and sugar in a bowl. Season and whisk together. Pour over the salad and cover all the leaves and fruit. Sprinkle with the chopped mint and serve immediately.

PREPARATION TIME: 10 MINUTES   COOKING TIME: NIL

Salmon and fennel salad

SOUTH-WESTERN BEAN SALAD

220 g (7³/4 oz/1 cup) dried black beans

200 g (7 oz/1 cup) dried cannellini beans

1 red onion

1 red capsicum (pepper), seeded and membrane removed

270 g (9¹/2 oz) tinned corn kernels, drained

3 tablespoons chopped coriander (cilantro) leaves

1 garlic clove, crushed

¹/2 teaspoon ground cumin

¹/2 teaspoon French mustard

2 tablespoons red wine vinegar

60 ml (2 fl oz/¹/4 cup) olive oil

SERVES 4–6

Soak the beans in separate bowls of cold water overnight. Drain the beans. Put them in separate saucepans and cover with water. Bring both pans to the boil, reduce the heat and simmer for 45 minutes, or until the beans are tender. Drain, rinse and allow to cool.

Slice the onion and red capsicum. Put in a bowl and add the beans, corn and coriander. Stir until well combined.

Combine the garlic, cumin, mustard and vinegar in a small bowl, then gradually whisk in the oil and lightly season. Pour over the bean mixture and toss lightly to combine.

PREPARATION TIME: 20 MINUTES +   COOKING TIME: 50 MINUTES

NOTE: This salad can be made up to a day in advance. Black beans are also known as turtle beans and are available at good delicatessens. They are not to be confused with Chinese black beans.

ROASTED FENNEL AND ORANGE SALAD

8 baby fennel bulbs
100 ml (3½ fl oz) olive oil
2 oranges
1 tablespoon lemon juice
1 red onion, halved and thinly sliced
100 g (3½ oz) kalamata olives
2 tablespoons roughly chopped mint
1 tablespoon roughly chopped flat-leaf (Italian) parsley

SERVES 4

Preheat the oven to 200°C (400°F/Gas 6). Trim the fronds from the fennel and reserve. Remove the stalks and cut a slice off the base of each fennel about 5 mm (¼ inch) thick. Slice each fennel into six wedges, put in an ovenproof dish and drizzle with 60 ml (2 fl oz/¼ cup) of the olive oil. Season well. Bake for 40–45 minutes, or until the fennel is tender and slightly caramelized. Turn once or twice during cooking. Allow to cool.

Cut a thin slice off the top and bottom of each orange. Using a small, sharp knife, slice the skin and pith off the oranges. Remove as much pith as possible. Slice down the side of a segment between the flesh and the membrane. Repeat with the other side and lift the segment out. Do this over a bowl to catch the juices. Repeat with all the segments on both oranges. Squeeze out any juice remaining in the membranes.

Whisk the remaining oil into the orange juice and lemon juice until emulsified. Season well. Combine the orange segments, onion and olives in a bowl, pour over half the dressing and add half the mint. Mix well. Transfer to a serving dish. Top with the roasted fennel, drizzle with the remaining dressing and scatter the parsley and remaining mint over the top. Chop the reserved fronds and sprinkle over the salad.

PREPARATION TIME: 30 MINUTES   COOKING TIME: 45 MINUTES

PIQUANT POTATO SALAD

500 g (1 lb 2 oz) small boiling potatoes
2 teaspoons chopped dill
2 spring onions (scallions), chopped
1 tablespoon capers, rinsed and squeezed dry, roughly chopped
2 tablespoons extra virgin olive oil
1½ tablespoons lemon juice
1 teaspoon finely grated orange zest

SERVES 4

Put the potatoes in a large saucepan of salted water and bring to the boil. Cook for 10 minutes, or until tender when pierced with a knife. Drain well.

Put the potatoes in a bowl with the dill, spring onion and capers, and season. Mix well to combine. Whisk together the oil, lemon juice and orange zest in a small bowl and pour over the hot potatoes. Toss to coat the potatoes and serve warm.

PREPARATION TIME: 10 MINUTES   COOKING TIME: 15 MINUTES

Roasted fennel and orange salad

CRAB AND MANGO SALAD

DRESSING
80 ml (2½ fl oz/⅓ cup) light olive oil
60 ml (2 fl oz/¼ cup) lime juice
1 teaspoon fish sauce
½ small green chilli, finely chopped
1 tablespoon finely chopped coriander
(cilantro) leaves
2 teaspoons grated fresh ginger

two 4 cm (1½ inch) squares fresh
coconut
1 teaspoon olive oil
60 g (2¼ oz/2 cups) watercress, trimmed
100 g (3½ oz) snow pea (mangetout)
sprouts
100 g (3½ oz) small cooked prawns
(shrimp)
400 g (14 oz) cooked fresh or tinned
crabmeat, drained if tinned
1 firm mango, cut into thin strips
coriander (cilantro) leaves, to garnish
1 lime, cut into slices, to garnish

SERVES 4

To make the dressing, combine all the ingredients and season. Set aside to allow the flavours to infuse.

Peel the coconut into wafer-thin slices with a vegetable peeler. Heat the olive oil in a frying pan and gently fry the coconut, stirring, until golden. Drain on crumpled paper towels.

Combine the watercress and snow pea sprouts and arrange on a platter.

Peel the prawns, leaving the tails intact. Gently pull out the dark vein from each prawn back, starting at the head end. Lightly toss the crabmeat, prawns, mango and three-quarters of the toasted coconut and dressing together. Pile in the centre of the watercress and snow pea sprout mixture, scatter the remaining coconut over the top and garnish with the coriander leaves and lime slices.

PREPARATION TIME: 25 MINUTES   COOKING TIME: 5 MINUTES

NOTE: If you can't get fresh coconut, use 30 g (1 oz/½ cup) flaked coconut and toast it.

FATTOUSH

2 pitta bread rounds (17 cm/16½ inch diameter)
1 large Lebanese (short) cucumber
6 cos (romaine) lettuce leaves, shredded
4 tomatoes, cut into 1 cm (½ inch) cubes
8 spring onions (scallions), chopped
4 tablespoons chopped flat-leaf (Italian) parsley
1 tablespoon chopped mint
2 tablespoons chopped coriander (cilantro) leaves

DRESSING
2 garlic cloves, crushed
100 ml (3½ fl oz) extra virgin olive oil
100 ml (3½ fl oz) lemon juice

SERVES 6

Preheat the oven to 180°C (350°F/Gas 4). Split each pitta bread into two rounds through the centre and bake for about 8 minutes, or until golden and crisp, turning halfway through. Break into small pieces.

To make the dressing, whisk all of the ingredients together in a bowl until well combined.

Cut the cucumber into 1 cm (½ inch) cubes. Put the cucumber, bread pieces and remaining salad ingredients in a bowl and toss. Pour on the dressing and toss well. Season to taste and serve immediately.

PREPARATION TIME: 15 MINUTES COOKING TIME: 10 MINUTES

FRESH BEETROOT AND GOAT'S CHEESE SALAD

1 kg (2 lb 4 oz) fresh beetroot (beets) (4 bulbs with leaves)
200 g (7 oz) green beans, trimmed
1 tablespoon red wine vinegar
2 tablespoons extra virgin olive oil
1 garlic clove, crushed
1 tablespoon capers, rinsed and squeezed dry, roughly chopped
100 g (3½ oz) goat's cheese

SERVES 4

Trim the leaves from the beetroot, scrub the bulbs and wash the leaves. Put the bulbs in a large saucepan of salted water, bring to the boil, then reduce the heat, cover and simmer for 30 minutes, or until tender.

Meanwhile, bring a saucepan of water to the boil, add the beans and cook for 3 minutes, or until just tender. Remove with a slotted spoon and plunge into a bowl of cold water. Drain well. Add the beetroot leaves to the same pan of water and cook for 3–5 minutes, or until the leaves and stems are tender. Drain, plunge into a bowl of cold water, then drain well. Drain and cool the beetroots, peel the skins off and cut into thin wedges.

To make the dressing, mix the vinegar, oil, garlic, capers and ½ teaspoon each of salt and pepper. Divide the beans, beetroot leaves and bulbs among four serving plates. Crumble the goat's cheese over the top of each and drizzle with dressing. Delicious served with fresh crusty bread.

PREPARATION TIME: 20 MINUTES COOKING TIME: 30 MINUTES

CIRCASSIAN CHICKEN

2 teaspoons paprika

$1/4$ teaspoon cayenne pepper

1 tablespoon walnut oil

4 chicken breast, on the bone

4 chicken wings

1 large onion, chopped

2 celery stalks, roughly chopped

1 carrot, chopped

1 bay leaf

4 sprigs flat-leaf (Italian) parsley

1 sprig thyme

6 peppercorns

1 teaspoon coriander seeds

250 g (9 oz/$2^1/2$ cups) walnuts, toasted (see Note)

2 slices white bread, crusts removed

4 garlic cloves, crushed

1 tablespoon paprika, extra

salad leaves, to serve

SERVES 6

Put the paprika and cayenne pepper in a small dry frying pan and heat over low heat for about 2 minutes, or until aromatic. Add the walnut oil to the pan and set aside until ready to use.

Put the chicken pieces in a large saucepan with the onion, celery, carrot, bay leaf, parsley, thyme, peppercorns and coriander seeds. Add 1 litre (35 fl oz/4 cups) water and bring to the boil. Reduce the heat to low and simmer for 15–20 minutes, or until the chicken is tender. Remove from the heat and allow to cool in the stock. Remove the chicken pieces and return the stock to the heat. Simmer for 20–25 minutes, or until reduced by half. Strain, skim off the fat and reserve the stock. Remove the chicken skin and shred the flesh into bite-sized pieces. Season well and ladle some stock over the chicken to keep it moist. Set aside.

Reserve a few of the walnuts to use as a garnish and blend the rest in a food processor to form a rough paste. Combine the bread with 125 ml (4 fl oz/$1/2$ cup) of the reserved stock, add to the food processor and mix in short bursts for several seconds. Add the garlic and extra paprika, and season. Process until smooth. Gradually add 250 ml (9 fl oz/1 cup) of warm chicken stock until the mixture is of a smooth pourable consistency, adding a little more stock if necessary.

Mix half the sauce with the chicken and place on a serving platter. Pour the rest over to cover, then sprinkle with the spiced walnut oil and the remaining walnuts. Serve at room temperature on a bed of salad leaves.

PREPARATION TIME: 25 MINUTES   COOKING TIME: 1 HOUR

NOTE: Californian walnuts are best for this recipe as they are much less bitter than other types of walnuts.

ASPARAGUS VINAIGRETTE

2 teaspoons dijon mustard
2 tablespoons sherry vinegar
80 ml (2$\frac{1}{2}$ fl oz/$\frac{1}{3}$ cup) extra virgin olive oil
$\frac{1}{2}$ teaspoon finely snipped chives
24 asparagus spears, woody ends trimmed
60 ml (2 fl oz/$\frac{1}{4}$ cup) olive oil
2 garlic cloves, peeled
80 g (2$\frac{3}{4}$ oz/1 cup) fresh breadcrumbs

SERVES 4

To make the vinaigrette, whisk together the mustard, sherry vinegar, extra virgin olive oil and chives in a small bowl.

Cook the asparagus spears in a large saucepan of boiling salted water over medium heat for 2–4 minutes, or until just tender.

While the asparagus is cooking, heat the olive oil in a frying pan, add the garlic and cook over low heat until golden. Discard the garlic, then add the breadcrumbs and increase the heat to medium. Cook until the breadcrumbs are crisp and golden. Season and drain on paper towels.

Drain the asparagus and place on a platter. Drizzle with the vinaigrette and sprinkle with breadcrumbs.

PREPARATION TIME: 10 MINUTES   COOKING TIME: 10 MINUTES

SUGAR SNAP PEAS AND CARROTS IN LIME BUTTER

60 g (2$\frac{1}{4}$ oz) butter
2 garlic cloves, crushed
1 tablespoon lime juice and peel from 1 lime
$\frac{1}{2}$ teaspoon soft brown sugar
125 g (4$\frac{1}{2}$ oz) carrots, cut into thin slices, diagonally
125 g (4$\frac{1}{2}$ oz) sugar snap peas, strings removed

SERVES 4

Heat the butter in a large, heavy-based frying pan. Add the garlic and cook over low heat for 1 minute. Add the lime juice and sugar and cook over low heat until the sugar has dissolved. Add the carrots and peas and cook over medium heat for 2–3 minutes, or until just cooked. Keep warm.

Peel the lime peel into long strips using a vegetable peeler. Remove all white pith. Cut into long, thin strips with a sharp knife. Serve the peas and carrots with the lime butter and garnish with the lime peel.

PREPARATION TIME: 15 MINUTES   COOKING TIME: 10 MINUTES

NOTE: Snow peas (mangetout) or green beans can be used in place of the peas. Baby carrots also make an attractive addition to this recipe — leave a portion of the green tops on. If limes are unavailable, substitute lemon juice and peel.

Asparagus vinaigrette

CHICKEN FALAFEL WITH TABOULEH CONES

45 g (1½ oz/¼ cup) burghul (bulgar)
4 pieces lavash or other unleavened bread (23 x 30 cm/9 x 12 inch)
2 spring onions (scallions), thinly sliced
1 large tomato, seeded and finely chopped
1 small Lebanese (short) cucumber, finely chopped
1 large handful flat-leaf (Italian) parsley, chopped
1 tablespoon lemon juice
1 tablespoon virgin olive oil
1 tablespoon olive oil
1 onion, finely chopped
1 garlic clove, crushed
2 teaspoons ground coriander
1 teaspoon cumin seeds
½ teaspoon ground cinnamon
250 g (9 oz) minced (ground) chicken
300 g (10½ oz) tinned chickpeas, rinsed, drained and mashed
1 handful mint, chopped
1 handful flat-leaf (Italian) parsley, extra, chopped
2 tablespoons plain (all-purpose) flour
vegetable oil, for frying
60 g (2¼ oz/¼ cup) Greek-style yoghurt

MAKES 24

Soak the burghul in hot water for 20 minutes. Slice the bread into thirds widthways, then cut in half. Keep the bread covered with a damp cloth to prevent it drying out. Cut 24 pieces of baking paper the same size as the bread. Roll the paper up around the bottom half of the bread to form a cone and secure. Twist at the bottom. You will need 24 bread cones.

To make the tabouleh, drain the burghul in a fine mesh sieve, pressing out as much water as possible. Transfer to a bowl and mix with the spring onion, tomato, cucumber, parsley, lemon juice and virgin olive oil, and season.

Heat the olive oil in a frying pan, add the onion and garlic and cook, stirring over medium–low heat, for 5 minutes, or until the onion is soft. Add the spices and cook for another minute, or until the spices are aromatic.

Put the onion mixture, minced chicken, chickpeas, mint and extra parsley in a bowl, season and mix until combined. Shape into 24 firm falafel patties. Toss the falafel in the flour and shake off the excess.

Fill a deep-fryer or heavy-based saucepan one-third full of oil and heat to 180°C (350°F), or until a cube of bread dropped into the oil turns golden brown in 15 seconds. Cook the falafels in batches for 3–4 minutes each side, or until golden and heated through. Drain on crumpled paper towels.

To assemble, put a falafel in each bread cone, top with tabouleh, then ½ teaspoon yoghurt.

PREPARATION TIME: 30 MINUTES +   COOKING TIME: 20 MINUTES

NOTE: The tabouleh is best made on the day of serving. The falafel can be prepared up to a day ahead and cooked just before serving.

BARBECUED OCTOPUS

170 ml (5½ fl oz/⅔ cup) olive oil
10 g (¼ oz) chopped oregano
3 tablespoons chopped flat-leaf (Italian) parsley
1 tablespoon lemon juice
3 small red chillies, seeded and finely chopped
3 garlic cloves, crushed
1 kg (2 lb 4 oz) baby octopus
lime wedges, to serve

SERVES 6

To make the marinade, combine the oil, herbs, lemon juice, chilli and garlic in a large bowl and mix well.

Use a small, sharp knife to remove the octopus heads. Grasp the bodies and push the beaks out from the centre with your index finger, then remove and discard. Slit the heads and remove the gut. If the octopus are too large, cut them into smaller portions.

Mix the octopus with the herb marinade. Cover and refrigerate for several hours, or overnight. Drain and reserve the marinade. Cook on a very hot, lightly oiled barbecue or in a very hot frying pan for 3–5 minutes, or until the flesh turns white. Turn frequently and brush generously with the marinade during cooking.

PREPARATION TIME: 15 MINUTES +   COOKING TIME: 5 MINUTES

GRILLED LAMB KOFTA

400 g (14 oz) minced (ground) lean lamb
1 tablespoon chopped flat-leaf (Italian) parsley
1 teaspoon ground cumin
2 tablespoons chopped coriander (cilantro) leaves
pinch cayenne pepper
2 garlic cloves, crushed
½ teaspoon dried mint
185 g (6½ oz/¾ cup) Greek-style yoghurt
lemon wedges, to serve

MAKES 8

Soak eight 15 cm (6 inch) wooden skewers in water for 30 minutes, to prevent them from burning during cooking.

To make the kofta, combine the minced lamb, parsley, cumin, coriander, cayenne pepper, half of the garlic and ½ teaspoon salt in a bowl and knead the mixture by hand for a few minutes until it is quite smooth and comes away easily from the side of the bowl. Divide the mixture into 16 portions. Wet your hands with cold water and roll each portion into a ball. Thread two balls onto each prepared skewer, moulding each ball into an oval shape about 4–5 cm (1½–2 inches) long.

To make the sauce, combine the dried mint, yoghurt and remaining garlic in a bowl and season.

Heat a lightly oiled barbecue hotplate until hot, or heat a grill (broiler) to its highest setting. Cook the kofta for about 6 minutes, turning once. Serve the kofta hot with the sauce for dipping and some lemon wedges.

PREPARATION TIME: 20 MINUTES +   COOKING TIME: 10 MINUTES

Barbecued octopus

TUNA SKEWERS WITH MOROCCAN SPICES AND CHERMOULA

800 g (1 lb 12 oz) tuna steaks
2 tablespoons olive oil
1/2 teaspoon ground cumin
2 teaspoons finely grated lemon zest

CHERMOULA
1/2 teaspoon ground coriander
3 teaspoons ground cumin
2 teaspoons paprika
pinch cayenne pepper
4 garlic cloves, crushed
15 g (1/2 oz) chopped flat-leaf
(Italian) parsley
25 g (3/4 oz) chopped
coriander (cilantro) leaves
80 ml (2 1/2 fl oz/1/3 cup) lemon juice
125 ml (4 fl oz/1/2 cup) olive oil

SERVES 4

If using wooden skewers, soak them for about 30 minutes to prevent them from burning during cooking.

Cut the tuna into 3 cm (1 1/4 inch) cubes and put in a shallow non-metallic dish. Combine the oil, cumin and lemon zest and pour over the tuna. Toss to coat, then cover and marinate in the refrigerator for 10 minutes.

Meanwhile, to make the chermoula, put the ground coriander, cumin, paprika and cayenne pepper in a small frying pan and cook over medium heat for 30 seconds, or until fragrant. Combine with the remaining chermoula ingredients and set aside.

Thread the tuna onto the skewers. Lightly oil a chargrill pan or barbecue and cook the skewers for 1 minute on each side for rare or 2 minutes for medium. Serve the skewers on a bed of couscous with the chermoula drizzled over the tuna.

PREPARATION TIME: 20 MINUTES +   COOKING TIME: 5 MINUTES

SKEWERED SWORDFISH WITH LEMON SAUCE

MARINADE
80 ml (2 1/2 fl oz/1/3 cup) lemon juice
2 tablespoons olive oil
1 small red onion, thinly sliced
1 teaspoon paprika
2 bay leaves, crushed
10 sage leaves, torn

1.5 kg (3 lb 5 oz) swordfish
3 tablespoons flat-leaf (Italian) parsley
60 ml (2 fl oz/1/4 cup) olive oil
60 ml (2 fl oz/1/4 cup) lemon juice

SERVES 6

Combine the marinade ingredients with 1 teaspoon salt and some ground black pepper in a bowl. Add the fish, toss to coat with the marinade, then cover and refrigerate for 3 hours, turning the fish occasionally.

Cut the fish into 3 cm (1 1/4 inch) cubes. Thread onto six metal skewers and cook over a chargrill pan or barbecue hotplate for 5 minutes, turning and brushing with marinade several times.

To make the lemon sauce, chop the parsley and combine with the oil and lemon juice. Serve over the fish.

PREPARATION TIME: 15 MINUTES +   COOKING TIME: 10 MINUTES

Tuna skewers with Moroccan spices and chermoula

BARBECUED FISH WITH ONIONS AND GINGER

1 kg (2 lb 4 oz) small whole firm white
fish, cleaned, gutted and scaled
2 teaspoons bottled green peppercorns,
drained and finely crushed
2 teaspoons chopped red chilli
3 teaspoons fish sauce
60 ml (2 fl oz/¼ cup) oil
2 onions, thinly sliced
4 cm (1½ inch) piece fresh ginger,
thinly sliced
3 garlic cloves, cut into very thin slivers
2 teaspoons sugar
4 spring onions (scallions), finely
shredded

LEMON AND GARLIC DIPPING SAUCE
60 ml (2 fl oz/¼ cup) lemon juice
2 tablespoons fish sauce
1 tablespoon sugar
2 small red chillies, finely chopped
3 garlic cloves, chopped

SERVES 4–6

Wash the fish and pat dry inside and out. Cut two or three diagonal slashes into the thickest part on both sides. In a food processor, process the peppercorns, chilli and fish sauce to a paste and brush over the fish. Refrigerate for 20 minutes.

Heat a barbecue hotplate or grill (broiler) until very hot and then brush with 1 tablespoon of the oil. Cook the fish for 8 minutes each side, or until the flesh flakes easily. If grilling (broiling), don't cook too close to the heat.

While the fish is cooking, heat the remaining oil in a frying pan and stir the onion over medium heat until golden. Add the ginger, garlic and sugar and cook for 3 minutes. Serve over the fish. Sprinkle with spring onion.

Stir all the dipping sauce ingredients in a bowl until the sugar has dissolved. Serve with the fish.

PREPARATION TIME: 25 MINUTES +   COOKING TIME: 25 MINUTES

SHISH KEBABS WITH CAPSICUM AND HERBS

1 kg (2 lb 4 oz) boneless leg of lamb
1 red capsicum (pepper)
1 green capsicum (pepper)
3 red onions
olive oil, for brushing

MARINADE
1 onion, thinly sliced
2 garlic cloves, crushed
60 ml (2 fl oz/¼ cup) lemon juice
80 ml (2½ fl oz/⅓ cup) olive oil
1 tablespoon chopped thyme
1 tablespoon paprika
½ teaspoon chilli flakes
2 teaspoons ground cumin
15 g (½ oz) chopped flat-leaf
(Italian) parsley
20 g (¾ oz) chopped mint

SERVES 4

If using wooden skewers, soak them for about 30 minutes to prevent them from burning during cooking.

Trim the sinew and most of the fat from the lamb and cut the meat into 3 cm (1¼ inch) cubes. Mix all the ingredients for the marinade in a large bowl. Season well, add the meat and mix well. Cover and refrigerate for 4–6 hours, or overnight.

Remove the seeds and membrane from the capsicums and cut the flesh into 3 cm (1¼ inch) squares. Cut each red onion into six wedges. Remove the lamb from the marinade and reserve the liquid. Thread the meat onto the skewers, alternating with onion and capsicum pieces. Grill (broil) the skewers for 5–6 minutes, brushing frequently with the marinade for the first couple of minutes. Serve immediately. These are delicious served with bread or pilaff.

PREPARATION TIME: 20 MINUTES +   COOKING TIME: 5 MINUTES

CHICKEN TIKKA SKEWERS

750 g (1 lb 10 oz) boneless, skinless
chicken thighs
¼ onion, chopped
2 garlic cloves, crushed
1 tablespoon grated fresh ginger
2 tablespoons lemon juice
3 teaspoons ground coriander
3 teaspoons ground cumin
3 teaspoons garam masala
90 g (3¼ oz/⅓ cup) plain yoghurt

MAKES 25–30

If using wooden skewers, soak them for about 30 minutes to prevent them from burning during cooking. Cut the chicken into 3 cm (1¼ inch) cubes.

Put the onion, garlic, ginger, lemon juice and spices in a food processor and finely chop. Transfer to a bowl and stir in the yoghurt and ½ teaspoon salt. Thread four pieces of chicken onto each skewer and put in a large ovenproof dish. Coat the chicken with the spice mixture. Cover and refrigerate for several hours, or overnight.

Barbecue, pan-fry or grill (broil) the chicken skewers, turning frequently, until cooked through.

PREPARATION TIME: 30 MINUTES +   COOKING TIME: 15 MINUTES

NOTE: Skewered chicken can be left to marinate in the refrigerator for 1–2 days.

Shish kebabs with capsicum and herbs

MILLEFEUILLE WITH PASSIONFRUIT CURD

PASSIONFRUIT CURD
3 eggs
60 g (2¼ oz) unsalted butter
125 g (4½ oz/½ cup) passionfruit pulp
110 g (3¾ oz/½ cup) sugar

500 g (1 lb 2 oz) block ready-made puff
pastry, thawed
300 ml (10½ fl oz) pouring (whipping)
cream
2 tablespoons icing (confectioners') sugar
1 teaspoon natural vanilla extract
1 large mango, thinly sliced
sifted icing (confectioners') sugar, extra
to sprinkle

SERVES 4

To make the passionfruit curd, beat the eggs well, then strain into a heatproof bowl and add the remaining ingredients. Place the bowl over a saucepan of simmering water and stir with a wooden spoon for 15–20 minutes, or until the butter has melted and the mixture has thickened slightly and coats the back of the wooden spoon. Cool, then transfer to a bowl, cover with plastic wrap and chill until required.

To make the millefeuille, preheat the oven to 200°C (400°F/Gas 6). Line a large baking tray with baking paper. Roll the pastry to a 30 x 35 cm (12 x 14 inch) rectangle and transfer to the tray. Cover and refrigerate for 20 minutes. Sprinkle lightly with water and prick all over with a fork. Cook for 25 minutes, or until puffed and golden. Allow to cool completely on a wire rack.

Whisk the cream with the icing sugar and vanilla extract until firm peaks form. Carefully trim the pastry sheet and cut into three even-sized strips, lengthways. Spread one layer of pastry with half the passionfruit curd, spreading evenly to the edges. Top this with half of the whipped cream and then top with half of the mango flesh. Place a second sheet of pastry on top and repeat the process. Top with the remaining pastry sheet and sprinkle liberally with icing sugar. Carefully transfer to a serving plate. Use a serrated knife to cut into slices.

PREPARATION TIME: 30 MINUTES +   COOKING TIME: 45 MINUTES

NOTE: Instead of making one long millefeuille, you might prefer to make four individual ones.

LEMON AND LIME SORBET

220 g (7³/₄ oz/1 cup) sugar
185 ml (6 fl oz/³/₄ cup) lemon juice
185 ml (6 fl oz/³/₄ cup) lime juice
2 egg whites, lightly beaten

SERVES 4

Stir 500 ml (17 fl oz/2 cups) water with the sugar in a saucepan, over low heat, until the sugar has dissolved. Bring to the boil, reduce the heat to low and simmer for 5 minutes. Cool. Add the lemon and lime juice to the syrup.

Transfer to an ice cream machine and freeze according to manufacturer's instructions. Add the egg white when the sorbet is almost churned and the machine is still running.

Alternatively, transfer to a shallow metal tray, Cover with a piece of baking paper and freeze for 2 hours. Transfer the icy mixture to a food processor or bowl and process or beat with electric beaters to a slush, then return to the freezer. Repeat the beating and freezing twice more. Transfer to a bowl or food processor. With electric beaters or with the processor's motor running, add the egg whites and blend. Return to the freezer container, cover with a piece of baking paper and freeze until firm.

PREPARATION TIME: 25 MINUTES + COOKING TIME: 10 MINUTES

FRUIT KEBABS WITH HONEY CARDAMOM SYRUP

¹/₄ small pineapple or 2 rings tinned pineapple
1 peach
1 banana
16 strawberries
pouring (whipping) cream or yoghurt, to serve (optional)

HONEY CARDAMOM SYRUP
2 tablespoons honey
20 g (³/₄ oz) unsalted butter, melted
¹/₂ teaspoon ground cardamom
1 tablespoon rum or brandy (optional)
1 tablespoon soft brown sugar

MAKES 8

Soak eight wooden skewers in cold water for 30 minutes to prevent them burning during cooking. Cut the pineapple into eight bite-sized pieces. Cut the peach into eight wedges and slice the banana. Thread the fruit alternately on skewers and place in a shallow dish.

To make the honey cardamom syrup, combine all the ingredients in a bowl. Pour the mixture over the kebabs and brush to coat. Cover and leave to stand at room temperature for 1 hour. Prepare and heat a barbecue or grill (broiler).

Cook the kebabs on the hot, lightly greased barbecue or under the grill for 5 minutes. Brush with the syrup occasionally during cooking. Serve drizzled with the remaining syrup, and cream or yoghurt (if desired).

PREPARATION TIME: 20 MINUTES + COOKING TIME: 5 MINUTES

Lemon and lime sorbet

PAVLOVA ROLL WITH RASPBERRY COULIS

4 egg whites
230 g (8½ oz/1 cup) caster
(superfine) sugar
1 teaspoon cornflour (cornstarch)
2 teaspoons lemon juice or white vinegar
170 ml (5½ fl oz/⅔ cup) whipped cream
55 g (2 oz/¼ cup) chopped fresh berries

RASPBERRY COULIS
2 tablespoons brandy
250 g (9 oz/2 cups) fresh raspberries
1 tablespoon icing (confectioners') sugar

SERVES 8–10

Brush a 25 x 30 cm (10 x 12 inch) Swiss roll (jelly roll) tin with oil and line with baking paper extending up two sides. Preheat the oven to 180°C (350°F/Gas 4). Beat the egg whites into soft peaks, then gradually add 170 g (6 oz/¾ cup) of the sugar and beat until thick and glossy. Combine 1 tablespoon of the sugar with the cornflour. Fold into the meringue with the lemon juice or vinegar. Spoon into the tin and smooth. Bake for 12–15 minutes, or until springy.

Put a large sheet of baking paper on top of a tea towel (dish towel) and generously sprinkle with the rest of the sugar. Turn the pavlova onto the baking paper, peel off the lining paper and leave for 3 minutes. Roll up the pavlova from the long side using the tea towel to assist, then cool.

Fold the berries into the whipped cream. Unroll the pavlova, fill with the cream mixture and re-roll without the tea towel and baking paper. Transfer to a plate and refrigerate.

To make the raspberry coulis, put the brandy, raspberries and icing sugar in a food processor and process until well blended. Serve the pavlova roll in slices with the raspberry coulis.

PREPARATION TIME: 25 MINUTES +   COOKING TIME: 15 MINUTES

NOTE: If you prefer, a thick fruit purée may be used to fill the roll.

STRAWBERRIES ROMANOFF

750 g (1 lb 10 oz) strawberries, quartered
2 tablespoons Cointreau
1/4 teaspoon finely grated orange zest
1 tablespoon caster (superfine) sugar
125 ml (4 fl oz/1/2 cup) pouring (whipping) cream
2 tablespoons icing (confectioners') sugar

SERVES 4

Combine the strawberries, Cointreau, orange zest and caster sugar in a large bowl, cover and refrigerate for 1 hour. Drain the strawberries, reserving any juices. Purée about one-quarter of the berries with the reserved juices.

Divide the remaining berries among four glasses. Beat the cream and icing sugar until soft peaks form, then fold the berry purée through the whipped cream. Spoon the mixture over the top of the strawberries, cover and refrigerate until required.

PREPARATION TIME: 20 MINUTES +   COOKING TIME: NIL

MANGO ICE CREAM

400 g (14 oz) fresh mango flesh
125 g (4 1/2 oz/1/2 cup) caster (superfine) sugar
60 ml (2 fl oz/1/4 cup) mango or apricot nectar
250 ml (9 fl oz/1 cup) pouring (whipping) cream
mango slices, extra, to serve (optional)

SERVES 6

Put the mango in a food processor and process until smooth. Transfer the mango purée to a bowl and add the sugar and nectar. Stir until the sugar has dissolved.

Beat the cream in a small bowl until stiff peaks form and then gently fold it through the mango mixture.

Transfer to an ice cream machine and freeze according to manufacturer's instructions. Alternatively, transfer to a shallow metal tray and freeze, whisking every couple of hours until frozen and creamy. Freeze for 5 hours or overnight. Soften in the fridge for 30 minutes before serving with mango slices (if desired).

PREPARATION TIME: 20 MINUTES +   COOKING TIME: NIL

NOTE: Frozen or tinned mango can be used if fresh mango is not readily available.

Strawberries romanoff

WINTER WARMERS

CREAMY BAKED SCALLOPS

24 scallops, on the shell
250 ml (9 fl oz/1 cup) fish stock
250 ml (9 fl oz/1 cup) dry white wine
60 g (2¼ oz) butter
4 spring onions (scallions), chopped
1 bacon slice, finely chopped
100 g (3½ oz) button mushrooms,
thinly sliced
30 g (1 oz/¼ cup) plain (all-purpose) flour
185 ml (6 fl oz/¾ cup) pouring (whipping)
cream
1 teaspoon lemon juice
80 g (2¾ oz/1 cup) fresh breadcrumbs
30 g (1 oz) butter, extra, melted

SERVES 4

Slice or pull off any vein, membrane or hard white muscle from the scallops, leaving any roe attached. Remove the scallops from the shells and cut the scallops in half. Rinse and reserve the shells.

Heat the fish stock and white wine in a saucepan and add the scallops. Cover and simmer over medium heat for 2–3 minutes, or until the scallops are opaque and tender. Remove the scallops with a slotted spoon, cover and set aside. Bring the liquid in the pan to the boil and reduce until 375 ml (13 fl oz/1½ cups) remain.

Melt the butter in a saucepan and add the spring onion, bacon and mushrooms. Cook over medium heat for 3 minutes, stirring occasionally, until the onion is soft but not brown.

Stir in the flour and cook for 2 minutes. Remove from the heat and gradually stir in the reduced stock. Return to the heat and stir until the mixture boils and thickens. Reduce the heat and simmer for 2 minutes. Stir in the cream, lemon juice and season to taste. Cover, set aside and keep warm.

Combine the breadcrumbs and extra butter in a small bowl. Preheat the grill (broiler) to high.

Divide the scallops among the shells. Spoon the warm sauce over the scallops and sprinkle with the breadcrumb mixture. Place under the grill until the breadcrumbs are golden brown. Serve immediately.

PREPARATION TIME: 20 MINUTES   COOKING TIME: 10 MINUTES

CLAMS IN WHITE WINE

1 kg (2 lb 4 oz) clams (vongole) (see Note)
2 large tomatoes
2 tablespoons olive oil
1 small onion, finely chopped
2 garlic cloves, crushed
1 tablespoon chopped flat-leaf
(Italian) parsley
pinch freshly grated nutmeg
80 ml (2½ fl oz/⅓ cup) dry white wine
flat-leaf (Italian) parsley, to garnish

SERVES 4

Soak the clams in salted water for 1 hour to release any grit. Rinse under running water and discard any open clams. Score a cross in the base of each tomato. Put in a heatproof bowl and cover with boiling water. Leave for 30 seconds, then transfer to cold water and peel the skin away from the cross. Cut the tomatoes in half, scoop out the seeds and finely chop.

Heat the oil in a large flameproof casserole dish and cook the onion over low heat for 5 minutes, or until softened. Add the garlic and tomato and cook for 5 minutes. Stir in the parsley and nutmeg and season. Add 80 ml (2½ fl oz/⅓ cup) water.

Add the clams and cook over low heat until they open. Discard any that don't open. Add the wine and cook over low heat for 3–4 minutes, or until the sauce thickens, gently moving the dish back and forth a few times, rather than stirring the clams, so that the clams stay in the shells. Serve at once, with bread.

PREPARATION TIME: 10 MINUTES +   COOKING TIME: 20 MINUTES

NOTE: You can use mussels instead of clams in this recipe.

CHEESE TRIANGLES

250 g (9 oz) Greek feta cheese
185 g (6½ oz) gruyère cheese, grated
2 eggs, lightly beaten
white pepper, to taste
15 sheets filo pastry, halved widthways
125 ml (4 fl oz/½ cup) olive oil
125 g (4½ oz) butter, melted

MAKES 30

Preheat the oven to 180°C (350°F/Gas 4). Put the feta in a bowl and mash with a fork. Add the gruyère, egg and pepper and mix.

Keep one half of the pastry covered with a damp tea towel (dish towel) to prevent it drying out. Place one half of one sheet of pastry lengthways on a work surface. Brush with the combined oil and butter, then fold into thirds lengthways. Brush with the oil and butter. Put 1 tablespoon of cheese mixture on the corner of the pastry strip. Fold this corner over the filling to the edge of the pastry to form a triangle. Continue to fold until the filling is enclosed and the end of pastry is reached. Repeat with the remaining pastry and filling.

Place the triangles on a lightly greased baking tray and brush them with the oil and butter mixture. Bake for 20 minutes, or until crisp.

PREPARATION TIME: 35 MINUTES   COOKING TIME: 20 MINUTES

Clams in white wine

HAM AND MUSHROOM CROQUETTES

90 g (3½ oz) butter
1 small onion, finely chopped
110 g (3¾ oz) cap mushrooms, finely chopped
90 g (3¼ oz/¾ cup) plain (all-purpose) flour
250 ml (9 fl oz/1 cup) milk
185 ml (6 fl oz/¾ cup) chicken stock
110 g (3¾ oz) ham, finely chopped
60 g (2¼ oz/½ cup) plain (all-purpose) flour, extra
2 eggs, lightly beaten
50 g (1¾ oz/½ cup) dry breadcrumbs
oil, for deep-frying

MAKES 18

Melt the butter in a saucepan over low heat, add the onion and cook for 5 minutes, or until translucent. Add the mushrooms and cook over low heat, stirring occasionally, for 5 minutes. Add the flour and stir over medium–low heat for 1 minute, or until the mixture is dry and crumbly and begins to change colour. Remove from the heat and gradually add the milk, stirring until smooth. Stir in the stock and return to the heat, stirring until the mixture boils and thickens. Stir in the ham and some black pepper, then transfer to a bowl to cool for about 2 hours.

Roll 2 tablespoons of mixture at a time into croquette shapes 6 cm (2½ inches) long. Put the extra flour, beaten egg and breadcrumbs in three shallow bowls. Toss the croquettes in the flour, dip in the egg, allowing the excess to drain away, then roll in the breadcrumbs. Place on a baking tray and refrigerate for about 30 minutes.

Fill a deep-fryer or heavy-based saucepan one-third full of oil and heat to 180°C (350°F), or until a cube of bread dropped into the oil browns in 15 seconds. Deep-fry the croquettes, in batches, for 3 minutes, turning, until brown. Drain well.

PREPARATION TIME: 35 MINUTES +   COOKING TIME: 20 MINUTES

NOTE: You can vary these croquettes very easily to suit your taste. For example, they are delicious if you replace the ham with finely chopped chicken or flaked cooked fish and add finely chopped herbs.

STUFFED TOMATOES

8 tomatoes
110 g (3³/₄ oz/¹/₂ cup) short-grain
white rice
2 tablespoons olive oil
1 red onion, chopped
1 garlic clove, crushed
1 teaspoon dried oregano
40 g (1¹/₂ oz/¹/₄ cup) pine nuts
35 g (1¹/₄ oz/¹/₄ cup) currants
30 g (1 oz) chopped basil
2 tablespoons chopped flat-leaf
(Italian) parsley
1 tablespoon chopped dill
olive oil, to brush

MAKES 8

Preheat the oven to 160°C (315°F/Gas 2–3). Lightly grease a large ovenproof dish. Slice the top off each tomato. Reserve the tops. Spoon out the flesh into a strainer over a bowl. Strain the juice into the bowl. Finely dice the flesh and reserve in a separate bowl. Drain the tomato shells upside down on a rack. Boil the rice in a saucepan of lightly salted water for 10–12 minutes, or until just tender. Drain and set aside to cool.

Heat the oil in a saucepan. Fry the onion, garlic and oregano for 8 minutes, or until the onion is soft. Add the pine nuts and currants and cook for 5 minutes, stirring frequently. Remove from the heat and stir in the herbs. Season. Add the onion mixture and reserved tomato pulp to the rice and mix well. Fill up the tomato shells with the rice mixture. Spoon 1 tablespoon of the reserved tomato juice on top of each tomato and replace the tops. Lightly brush the tomatoes with the oil and place them in the ovenproof dish. Bake for about 30 minutes, or until heated through.

PREPARATION TIME: 40 MINUTES   COOKING TIME: 55 MINUTES

PRAWN CROUSTADE

¹/₂ loaf unsliced white bread, crust
removed
125 ml (4 fl oz/¹/₂ cup) olive oil
1 garlic clove, crushed

FILLING
500 g (1 lb 2 oz) raw prawns (shrimp)
375 ml (13 fl oz/1¹/₂ cups) fish stock
2 slices lemon
50 g (1³/₄ oz) butter
6 spring onions (scallions), chopped
30 g (1 oz/¹/₄ cup) plain (all-purpose) flour
1 tablespoon lemon juice
¹/₂–1 teaspoon chopped dill
60 ml (2 fl oz/¹/₄ cup) pouring (whipping)
cream

SERVES 6

Preheat the oven to 210°C (415°F/Gas 6–7). Cut the bread into slices 5 cm (2 inches) thick. Cut each slice diagonally to form triangles. Cut another triangle 1 cm (¹/₂ inch) inside each piece without cutting all the way through, then scoop out the centres to create cavities for the filling, leaving a base on each. Heat the oil and garlic in a frying pan, brush all over the bread cases, then bake for 10 minutes, or until golden brown.

To make the filling, peel the prawns and gently pull out the dark vein from each prawn back, starting at the head end. Roughly chop the prawns, put in a small saucepan and cover with the stock. Add the lemon slices, simmer for 15 minutes, strain and reserve the liquid and prawns separately. Melt the butter in a saucepan, add the onion and stir over medium heat until soft. Stir in the flour and some pepper and cook for 2 minutes. Remove from the heat and gradually stir in the reserved prawn liquid. Return to the heat and stir over medium heat for 5 minutes, or until the sauce boils and thickens. Add the lemon juice, dill, cream and prawns, and stir until heated through. To serve, spoon the filling into the warm bread cases.

PREPARATION TIME: 45 MINUTES   COOKING TIME: 25 MINUTES

Stuffed tomatoes

CHEESE-FILLED CREPES WITH TOMATO SAUCE

CREPES
165 g (5³/4 oz/1¹/3 cups) plain (all-purpose) flour
500 ml (17 fl oz/2 cups) milk
3 eggs, lightly beaten
30 g (1 oz) butter, melted

TOMATO SAUCE
2 tablespoons oil
1 garlic clove, crushed
400 g (14 oz) tinned crushed tomatoes
3 tablespoons chopped flat-leaf (Italian) parsley

CHEESE FILLING
400 g (14 oz) ricotta cheese, crumbled
100 g (3¹/2 oz/²/3 cup) grated mozzarella cheese
25 g (1 oz/¹/4 cup) freshly grated parmesan cheese
pinch freshly grated nutmeg
3 tablespoons chopped flat-leaf (Italian) parsley

25 g (1 oz/¹/4 cup) freshly grated parmesan cheese
2 tablespoons extra virgin olive oil, to drizzle

MAKES ABOUT 12

To make the crepes, sift the flour and ¹/2 teaspoon salt into a bowl. Make a well in the centre and add the milk gradually, stirring constantly until the mixture is smooth. Add the eggs, little by little, beating well until smooth. Cover and set aside for 30 minutes.

Meanwhile, to make the tomato sauce, heat the oil in a heavy-based frying pan and add the garlic. Cook for 30 seconds over low heat until just golden, then add the tomatoes and 125 ml (4 fl oz/¹/2 cup) water and season well. Simmer over low heat for 30 minutes, or until the sauce has reduced and thickened. Stir in the parsley.

Heat a crepe pan or non-stick frying pan and brush lightly with the melted butter. Pour 60 ml (2 fl oz/¹/4 cup) of batter into the pan, swirling quickly to thinly cover the base. Cook for 1 minute, or until the underside is golden. Turn and cook the other side until golden. Transfer to a plate and continue with the remaining batter, stacking the crepes as you go.

Preheat the oven to 200°C (400°F/Gas 6) and lightly grease a shallow ovenproof dish with butter or oil.

To make the filling, mix all the ingredients together and season well.

To assemble, spread 1 heaped tablespoon of filling over each crepe, leaving a 1 cm (¹/2 inch) border. Fold the crepe in half and then in quarters. Place in the ovenproof dish, so that they overlap but are not crowded. Spoon the tomato sauce over the crepes, sprinkle with parmesan and drizzle with the extra virgin olive oil. Bake for 20 minutes, or until heated.

PREPARATION TIME: 25 MINUTES +   COOKING TIME: 1 HOUR 10 MINUTES

NOTE: The crepes can be made up to 3 days in advance but must be refrigerated with baking paper to separate them.

CHORIZO IN CIDER

3 teaspoons olive oil
1 small onion, finely chopped
1½ teaspoons paprika
125 ml (4 fl oz/½ cup) dry alcoholic
apple cider
60 ml (2 fl oz/¼ cup) chicken stock
1 bay leaf
280 g (10 oz) chorizo, sliced diagonally
2 teaspoons sherry vinegar, or to taste
2 teaspoons chopped flat-leaf
(Italian) parsley

SERVES 4

Heat the oil in a saucepan over low heat, then add the onion and cook for 3 minutes, stirring occasionally, or until soft. Add the paprika and cook for 1 minute.

Increase the heat to medium, add the apple cider, stock and bay leaf to the pan and bring to the boil. Reduce the heat and simmer for 5 minutes. Add the sliced chorizo and simmer for 5 minutes, or until the sauce has reduced slightly. Stir in the sherry vinegar and parsley. Serve hot.

PREPARATION TIME: 5 MINUTES   COOKING TIME: 15 MINUTES

SNAPPER PIES

2 tablespoons olive oil
4 onions, thinly sliced
375 ml (13 fl oz/1½ cups) fish stock
875 ml (30 fl oz/3½ cups) pouring
(whipping) cream
1 kg (2 lb 4 oz) skinless snapper fillets, cut
into large pieces
2 sheets frozen puff pastry, thawed
1 egg, lightly beaten

SERVES 4

Preheat the oven to 220°C (425°F/Gas 7). Heat the oil in a large deep-sided frying pan, add the onion and stir over medium heat for 20 minutes, or until the onion is golden brown and slightly caramelized.

Add the fish stock, bring to the boil and cook for 10 minutes, or until the liquid is nearly evaporated. Stir in the cream and bring to the boil. Reduce the heat and simmer for about 20 minutes, until the liquid is reduced by half, or until it coats the back of a spoon.

Divide half the sauce among four 500 ml (17 fl oz/2-cup) deep ramekins or dariole moulds. Put one-quarter of the fish in each ramekin, then top with some of the remaining sauce.

Cut the pastry sheets into rounds slightly larger than the tops of the ramekins. Brush the edges of the pastry with a little of the egg. Press onto the ramekins. Brush lightly with the remaining beaten egg. Bake for 30 minutes, or until crisp, golden and puffed.

PREPARATION TIME: 25 MINUTES   COOKING TIME: 1 HOUR 20 MINUTES

NOTE: You can substitute bream, sea perch or garfish for the snapper.

Chorizo in cider

CABBAGE ROLLS

1 tablespoon olive oil
1 onion, finely chopped
large pinch ground allspice
1 teaspoon ground cumin
large pinch freshly grated nutmeg
2 bay leaves
1 large head cabbage
500 g (1 lb 2 oz) minced (ground) lamb
220 g (7¾ oz/1 cup) short-grain white rice
4 garlic cloves, crushed
50 g (1¾ oz/⅓ cup) pine nuts, toasted
2 tablespoons chopped mint
2 tablespoons chopped flat-leaf
(Italian) parsley
1 tablespoon currants, chopped
250 ml (9 fl oz/1 cup) olive oil, extra
80 ml (2½ fl oz/⅓ cup) lemon juice
extra virgin olive oil, to drizzle
lemon wedges, to serve

MAKES 12 LARGE ROLLS

Heat the oil in a saucepan, add the onion and cook over medium heat for 10 minutes, or until golden. Add the allspice, cumin and nutmeg and cook for 2 minutes, or until fragrant. Remove from the pan.

Bring a very large saucepan of water to the boil and add the bay leaves. Cut the tough outer leaves and about 5 cm (2 inches) of the core from the cabbage, then carefully add the cabbage to the boiling water. Cook it for 5 minutes, then carefully loosen a whole leaf with tongs and remove. Continue to cook and remove the leaves until you reach the core. Drain, reserving the cooking liquid and set aside to cool.

Take 12 leaves of equal size and cut a small 'V' from the core end of each to remove the thickest part. Trim the firm central veins so the leaf is as flat as possible. Use three-quarters of the remaining leaves to line the base of a very large saucepan.

Combine the minced lamb, onion mixture, rice, garlic, pine nuts, mint, parsley and currants in a bowl and season well. With the core end of the leaf closest to you, form 2 tablespoons of the mixture into an oval and place in the centre of the leaf. Roll up, tucking in the sides. Repeat with the remaining 11 leaves and filling. Place tightly, in a single layer, in the lined saucepan, seam side down.

Combine 625 ml (21½ fl oz/2½ cups) of the reserved cooking liquid with the extra olive oil, lemon juice and 1 teaspoon salt and pour over the rolls (the liquid should just come to the top of the rolls). Lay the remaining cabbage leaves over the top. Cover and bring to the boil over high heat, then reduce the heat and simmer for 1¼ hours, or until the mince and rice are cooked. Carefully remove from the pan with a slotted spoon, then drizzle with the extra virgin olive oil. Serve with the lemon wedges.

PREPARATION TIME: 30 MINUTES   COOKING TIME: 1 HOUR 35 MINUTES

PROVENÇALE POTATO GALETTE

1 tablespoon olive oil
225 g (8 oz) bacon, finely chopped
2 onions, thinly sliced
2 teaspoons chopped thyme
500 g (1 lb 2 oz) all-purpose potatoes, thinly sliced
30 g (1 oz) butter
thyme sprigs, to garnish

SERVES 4–6

Preheat the oven to 180°C (350°F/Gas 4). Heat the oil in a frying pan and fry the bacon over medium heat until it starts to brown. Add the onion and thyme and cook for 3–4 minutes, or until softened. Transfer to a large bowl, add the potato, season and toss well.

Transfer the mixture to an 18 cm (7 inch) round cake tin and press down well. Dot with the butter. Put a piece of doubled baking paper over the top and place a weight, such as a ramekin or dariole mould or a smaller cake tin, over the paper. Bake for 40 minutes. Remove the weight and the paper and cook for another 20–25 minutes, or until the potato is tender and lightly golden. Leave to rest for 10 minutes. Run a knife around the edge of the tin and turn out the galette. Garnish with the thyme sprigs.

PREPARATION TIME: 10 MINUTES +   COOKING TIME: 1 HOUR 10 MINUTES

STUFFED ONIONS

8 onions (about 125 g/4$\frac{1}{2}$ oz each)
6 bacon slices, diced
4 garlic cloves, finely chopped
1 tablespoon pouring (whipping) cream
1 egg, lightly beaten
$\frac{1}{4}$ teaspoon freshly grated nutmeg
3 tablespoons chopped flat-leaf (Italian) parsley
60 g (2$\frac{1}{4}$ oz/$\frac{3}{4}$ cup) fresh breadcrumbs
2 tablespoons freshly grated parmesan cheese
40 g (1$\frac{1}{2}$ oz) butter, softened
250 ml (9 fl oz/1 cup) chicken stock

SERVES 4

Preheat the oven to 200°C (400°F/Gas 6). Lightly grease a shallow ovenproof dish.

Peel the onions, put them in a large saucepan of boiling water and simmer for 5–6 minutes. Remove the onions and drain well. Cool slightly and, using a small sharp knife, hollow out the centres, leaving a 1 cm ($\frac{1}{2}$ inch) rim. Reserve $\frac{1}{2}$ cup of the onion flesh from the centres. Season the onions.

Meanwhile, cook the bacon in a small frying pan over medium heat until the fat has melted. Chop the reserved onion centres and add to the pan with the garlic. Cook for 5 minutes, or until lightly golden. Remove from the heat, then add the cream, egg, nutmeg, parsley and 40 g (1$\frac{1}{2}$ oz/$\frac{1}{2}$ cup) of the crumbs. Season well and mix.

Spoon about 1–1$\frac{1}{2}$ tablespoons of the filling into the onion shells, piling a little to the top. Combine the remaining breadcrumbs with the parmesan, sprinkle over the onions and dot with the butter. Place in the greased dish and carefully pour the stock around the onions. Bake, basting occasionally, for 1 hour, or until the onions are tender.

PREPARATION TIME: 30 MINUTES   COOKING TIME: 1 HOUR 5 MINUTES

Provençale potato galette

VEGETABLE CASSEROLE

TOMATO SAUCE

1 kg (2 lb 4 oz) tomatoes
2 tablespoons olive oil
3 garlic cloves, crushed
1 red onion, finely chopped
2 teaspoons thyme, chopped

250 ml (9 fl oz/1 cup) olive oil
500 g (1 lb 2 oz) all-purpose potatoes,
cut into 5 mm (1/4 inch) rounds
500 g (1 lb 2 oz) eggplant (aubergine),
cut into 5 mm (1/4 inch) rounds
500 g (1 lb 2 oz) green capsicum
(pepper), seeded and membrane
removed, cut into 3 cm
(1¼ inch) pieces
10 g (1/4 oz/1/2 cup) flat-leaf (Italian)
parsley, roughly chopped

SERVES 6–8

To make the tomato sauce, score a cross in the base of each tomato. Put in a heatproof bowl and cover with boiling water. Leave for 30 seconds, then transfer to cold water and peel the skin away from the cross. Cut each tomato in half, scoop out the seeds and finely chop the flesh. Heat the oil in a heavy-based frying pan and cook the garlic and onion over low heat for 5–6 minutes, or until softened. Add the tomato and thyme and cook for 20 minutes over medium heat, or until thickened. Season to taste.

While the sauce is cooking, heat the oil in a heavy-based frying pan over low heat and cook the potato in batches until tender but not brown. Remove with a slotted spoon or tongs and place in a casserole dish measuring about 5 x 21 x 27 cm (2 x 8¼ x 10¾ inches). Lightly season.

Increase the heat to high and pan-fry the eggplant for 15 minutes, or until golden, turning after about 7 minutes. Drain the slices on paper towels, then place on top of the potatoes. Season lightly. Preheat the oven to 180°C (350°F/Gas 4).

Cook the capsicum in the same pan until tender but not browned, adding a little more olive oil if needed. Remove with a slotted spoon, drain on paper towels and arrange over the eggplant. Season lightly. Pour the tomato sauce over the top and bake for 20 minutes. Serve warm, sprinkled with parsley.

PREPARATION TIME: 30 MINUTES   COOKING TIME: 1 HOUR 10 MINUTES

SPICED BEEF AND ONION STEW

1 kg (2 lb 4 oz) chuck steak, trimmed of
excess fat and sinew
60 ml (2 fl oz/¼ cup) olive oil
750 g (1 lb 10 oz) baby onions
3 garlic cloves, halved lengthways
125 ml (4 fl oz/½ cup) red wine
1 cinnamon stick
4 whole cloves
1 bay leaf
1 tablespoon red wine vinegar
2 tablespoons tomato paste
(concentrated purée)
2 tablespoons currants

SERVES 4

Cut the meat into bite-sized cubes. Heat the oil over medium heat in a large heavy-based saucepan. Add the onions and stir for 5 minutes, or until golden. Remove from the pan and drain on paper towels. Add the meat to the pan and stir over high heat for 10 minutes, or until the meat is well browned and almost all the liquid has been absorbed.

Add the garlic, wine, spices, bay leaf, vinegar, tomato paste, ¼ teaspoon cracked black pepper, some salt and 375 ml (13 fl oz/1½ cups) water to the pan and bring to the boil. Reduce the heat, cover and simmer for 1 hour, stirring occasionally. Return the onions to the saucepan, add the currants and stir gently. Simmer, covered, for 15 minutes. Discard the cinnamon before serving. Delicious with rice, bread or potatoes.

PREPARATION TIME: 15 MINUTES   COOKING TIME: 1 HOUR 30 MINUTES

CHICKEN AND MUSHROOM RISOTTO

1.25 litres (44 fl oz/5 cups) vegetable or
chicken stock
2 tablespoons olive oil
300 g (10½ oz) boneless, skinless chicken
breast, cut into 1.5 cm (⅝ inch)
wide strips
250 g (9 oz) small button mushrooms, halved
pinch freshly grated nutmeg
2 garlic cloves, crushed
20 g (¾ oz) butter
1 small onion, finely chopped
360 g (12¾ oz/1⅔ cups) risotto rice
170 ml (5½ fl oz/⅔ cup) dry white wine
60 g (2¼ oz/¼ cup) sour cream
50 g (1¾ oz/½ cup) freshly grated
parmesan cheese
3 tablespoons chopped flat-leaf
(Italian) parsley

SERVES 4

Bring the stock to the boil over high heat, then reduce the heat and keep at a simmer. Heat the oil in a large saucepan. Cook the chicken over high heat for 3–4 minutes, or until golden brown. Add the mushrooms and cook for 1–2 minutes more, or until starting to brown. Stir in the nutmeg and garlic, and season. Cook for 30 seconds, then remove from the pan.

Melt the butter in the same pan and cook the onion over low heat for 5–6 minutes. Add the rice, stir to coat, then stir in the wine. Once the wine is absorbed, reduce the heat and add 125 ml (4 fl oz/½ cup) of the stock, stirring over medium heat until all the liquid is absorbed. Continue adding more liquid, 125 ml (4 fl oz/½ cup) at a time, until all the stock has been used and the rice is creamy. This will take about 20–25 minutes. Stir in the mushrooms and chicken with the last of the chicken stock.

Remove the pan from the heat and stir in the sour cream, parmesan and parsley. Season, then serve with a little extra parmesan.

PREPARATION TIME: 15 MINUTES   COOKING TIME: 45 MINUTES

Spiced beef and onion stew

CHICKEN AND ALMOND PILAFF

BAHARAT

1½ tablespoons coriander seeds

3 tablespoons black peppercorns

1½ tablespoons cassia bark

1½ tablespoons whole cloves

2 tablespoons cumin seeds

1 teaspoon cardamom seeds

2 whole nutmegs

3 tablespoons paprika

700 g (1 lb 9 oz) boneless, skinless chicken thighs, trimmed and cut into 3 cm (1¼ inch) wide strips

400 g (14 oz/2 cups) basmati rice

750 ml (26 fl oz/3 cups) chicken stock

2 tablespoons ghee

1 large onion, chopped

1 garlic clove, finely chopped

1 teaspoon ground turmeric

400 g (14 oz) tinned chopped tomatoes

1 cinnamon stick

4 cardamom pods, bruised

4 whole cloves

½ teaspoon finely grated lemon zest

3 tablespoons chopped coriander (cilantro) leaves

2 teaspoons lemon juice

40 g (1½ oz/⅓ cup) slivered almonds, toasted

SERVES 4–6

To make the baharat, grind the coriander seeds, peppercorns, cassia bark, cloves, cumin seeds and cardamom seeds to a powder using a mortar and pestle or in a spice grinder — you may need to do this in batches. Grate the nutmeg on the fine side of the grater and add to the spice mixture with the paprika. Stir together.

Combine the chicken and 1 tablespoon of the baharat in a large bowl, cover with plastic wrap and refrigerate for 1 hour. Meanwhile, put the rice in a large bowl, cover with cold water and soak for at least 30 minutes. Rinse under cold, running water until the water runs clear, then drain and set aside.

Bring the stock to the boil in a saucepan. Reduce the heat, cover and keep at a low simmer. Meanwhile, heat the ghee in a large, heavy-based saucepan over medium heat. Add the onion and garlic and cook for 5 minutes, or until soft and golden. Add the chicken and turmeric and cook for 5 minutes, or until browned. Add the rice and cook, stirring, for 2 minutes.

Add the tomatoes, simmering chicken stock, cinnamon stick, cardamom pods, cloves, lemon zest and 1 teaspoon salt. Stir well and bring to the boil, then reduce the heat to low and cover the saucepan with a tight-fitting lid. Simmer for 20 minutes, or until the stock is absorbed and the rice is cooked. Remove from the heat and allow to stand, covered, for 10 minutes.

Stir in the coriander, lemon juice and almonds. Season to taste.

PREPARATION TIME: 15 MINUTES +   COOKING TIME: 45 MINUTES

NOTE: Baharat is an aromatic spice blend used in Arabic cuisine to add depth of flavour to dishes such as soups, fish curries and tomato sauces. Baharat can be stored in an airtight jar for up to 3 months in a cool, dry place. It can be used in Middle Eastern casseroles and stews, rubbed on fish that is to be grilled (broiled), pan-fried or barbecued, or used with salt as a spice rub for lamb roasts, cutlets or chops.

PORK SAUSAGES WITH WHITE BEANS

350 g (12 oz/1¾ cups) dried white haricot beans
150 g (5½ oz) tocino, speck or pancetta, unsliced
½ leek, white part only, thinly sliced
2 garlic cloves
1 bay leaf
1 small red chilli, split and seeded
1 small onion
2 whole cloves
1 rosemary sprig
3 thyme sprigs
1 flat-leaf (Italian) parsley sprig
60 ml (2 fl oz/¼ cup) olive oil
8 pork sausages
½ onion, finely chopped
1 green capsicum (pepper), seeded and membrane removed, finely chopped
½ teaspoon paprika
125 ml (4 fl oz/½ cup) tomato passata (puréed tomatoes)
1 teaspoon cider vinegar

Soak the beans overnight in cold water. Drain and rinse the beans under cold water. Put them in a large saucepan with the tocino, leek, garlic, bay leaf and chilli. Stud the onion with the cloves and add to the pan. Tie the rosemary, thyme and parsley together and add to the pan. Pour in 750 ml (26 fl oz/3 cups) cold water and bring to the boil. Add 1 tablespoon of the oil, reduce the heat and simmer, covered, for 1 hour, or until the beans are tender. When necessary, add boiling water to keep the beans covered.

Prick each sausage five or six times and twist tightly in opposite directions in the middle to give two short fat sausages. Put in a single layer in a large frying pan and add enough cold water to reach halfway up their sides. Bring to the boil and simmer, turning a few times, until all the water has evaporated and the sausages brown lightly in the fat that is left in the pan. Remove from the pan and cut the short sausages apart. Add the remaining oil, the chopped onion and capsicum to the pan and fry over medium heat for 5–6 minutes. Stir in the paprika, cook for 30 seconds, then add the passata and season. Cook, stirring, for 1 minute.

Remove the tocino, herb sprigs and any loose large pieces of onion from the bean mixture. Leave in any loose leaves from the herbs, and any small pieces of onion. Add the sausages and sauce to the pan and stir the vinegar through. Bring to the boil. Adjust the seasoning.

SERVES 4   PREPARATION TIME: 25 MINUTES +   COOKING TIME: 1 HOUR 40 MINUTES

POACHED SALMON

375 ml (13 fl oz/1½ cups) fish stock
pinch freshly grated nutmeg
125 ml (4 fl oz/½ cup) dry white wine
2 spring onions (scallions), finely chopped
4 tail-end salmon steaks
3 tablespoons chopped flat-leaf (Italian) parsley
flat-leaf (Italian) parsley, extra, to garnish

Combine the stock, ½ teaspoon cracked black pepper, nutmeg, wine, spring onion and some salt in a frying pan and bring slowly to the boil for 1 minute. Put the salmon in the stock in a single layer. Cover and simmer for 8–10 minutes. Transfer the salmon to serving plates. Keep warm.

Boil the stock for another minute. Season to taste, then add the parsley. Spoon the liquid over the salmon and serve. Garnish with extra parsley.

PREPARATION TIME: 5 MINUTES +   COOKING TIME: 15 MINUTES

SERVES 4

Pork sausages with white beans

MEAT DUMPLINGS IN YOGHURT SAUCE

250 g (9 oz/2 cups) plain (all-purpose) flour
60 g (2¼ oz) clarified butter, melted, for baking (see Note)
40 g (1½ oz) clarified butter, extra, to serve
2 garlic cloves, crushed, to serve
1 tablespoon dried mint, to serve

FILLING
20 g (¾ oz) clarified butter
1 small onion, finely chopped
2 tablespoons pine nuts
250 g (9 oz) minced (ground) lamb
pinch ground allspice

YOGHURT SAUCE
750 g (1 lb 10 oz/3 cups) plain yoghurt
2 teaspoons cornflour (cornstarch)
1 egg white, lightly beaten

SERVES 4–6

To make the dough, sift the flour and 1 teaspoon salt into a bowl and add 185 ml (6 fl oz/¾ cup) water a little at a time and combine until the mixture comes together in a ball. Cover and allow to rest for 30 minutes.

To make the filling, melt the clarified butter in a deep heavy-based frying pan and cook the onion over medium heat for 5 minutes, or until soft. Add the pine nuts and allow them to brown, stirring constantly. Increase the heat to high and add the lamb and allspice, stirring until the meat changes colour. Season and allow to cool.

Preheat the oven to 180°C (350°F/Gas 4). Lightly grease two baking trays.

Roll out the dough on a floured board, to about 5 mm (¼ inch) thick and cut into rounds using a 5 cm (2 inch) cutter. Put a teaspoon of filling in the centre of each round and fold the pastry over into a crescent. Press the edges together firmly and then wrap the crescent around one finger and press the two ends together to make a hat shape. Place on the baking trays and brush lightly with the clarified butter. Bake for 10 minutes, or until lightly browned. The pastries do not have to be completely cooked.

To make the sauce, put the yoghurt in a large, heavy-based saucepan and stir until smooth. Combine the cornflour with 375 ml (13 fl oz/1½ cups) water, stir until smooth, then add to the yoghurt with the egg white and 2 teaspoons salt. Cook over medium heat, stirring constantly until the mixture thickens. Add the dumplings to the pan, stir very gently, then cook, uncovered, over low heat for 10 minutes, stirring occasionally. Be careful not to boil the sauce.

Just before serving, melt the extra clarified butter in a small frying pan and pan-fry the garlic gently for a few seconds. Stir in the mint and remove from the heat. Pour over the dumplings and serve with rice.

PREPARATION TIME: 40 MINUTES +   COOKING TIME: 35 MINUTES

NOTE: To clarify butter, heat a pack of butter over low heat until liquid. Leave until the white milk solids settle to the bottom. Use a spoon to skim off any foam, then strain off the golden liquid, leaving the white solids behind. Discard the solids.

VEAL COOKED WITH VINEGAR

60 g (2¼ oz/½ cup) plain (all-purpose) flour
large pinch cayenne pepper
1 kg (2 lb 4 oz) veal steaks
60 ml (2 fl oz/¼ cup) olive oil
1 bay leaf
5 garlic cloves, crushed
170 ml (5½ fl oz/⅔ cup) red wine vinegar
625 ml (21½ fl oz/2½ cups) beef stock
chopped flat-leaf (Italian) parsley, to garnish

SERVES 6–8

Combine the flour with the cayenne pepper and season well. Lightly coat the veal with the flour, shaking off any excess.

Heat the oil in a large, deep frying pan over high heat and cook the veal, a few pieces at a time, for 1 minute each side, or until lightly browned. Remove from the pan and set aside.

Add the bay leaf, garlic, red wine vinegar and stock to the pan and bring to the boil, scraping up any residue from the base of the pan. Reduce the heat to low and return the veal and any juices back to the pan. Cover and cook, stirring gently, occasionally, for 1½ hours, or until the veal is very tender and the sauce has thickened. If the sauce is too watery, carefully transfer the veal to a serving platter and boil the sauce until it is the consistency of a smooth gravy. Sprinkle with parsley before serving.

PREPARATION TIME: 10 MINUTES   COOKING TIME: 1 HOUR 50 MINUTES

ROAST LAMB WITH LEMON AND POTATOES

2.5–3 kg (5 lb 8 oz–6 lb 12 oz) leg of lamb
2 garlic cloves
125 ml (4 fl oz/½ cup) lemon juice
3 tablespoons dried oregano
1 onion, sliced
2 celery stalks, sliced
40 g (1¼ oz) butter, softened
1 kg (2 lb 4 oz) all-purpose potatoes, quartered

SERVES 6

Preheat the oven to 180°C (350°F/Gas 4). Cut small slits in the lamb and cut the garlic into slivers. Insert the garlic into the slits. Rub the entire surface with half the lemon juice, sprinkle with salt, pepper and half the oregano. Place in a roasting tin and roast for 1 hour.

Drain the fat from the pan. Add the onion, celery and 250 ml (9 fl oz/1 cup) hot water. Spread the butter over the lamb, reduce the oven to 160°C (315°F/Gas 2–3) and cook for 1 hour. Turn during cooking to brown evenly.

Add the potatoes to the pan, sprinkle with the remaining oregano, lemon juice and some salt and pepper. Bake for another hour, adding more water if required and turning the potatoes halfway through cooking. Cut the lamb into slices. Skim any excess fat from the pan and serve the juices with the potatoes and lamb.

PREPARATION TIME: 20 MINUTES   COOKING TIME: 3 HOURS

Veal cooked with vinegar

ROAST TURKEY WITH RICE AND CHESTNUT STUFFING

STUFFING

12 prunes, pitted

185 g (6¹/₂ oz) whole fresh chestnuts

40 g (1¹/₂ oz) butter

1 red onion, finely chopped

2 garlic cloves, crushed

60 g (2¹/₄ oz) pancetta (including any fat), finely chopped

100 g (3¹/₂ oz/¹/₂ cup) wild rice blend

60 ml (2 fl oz/¹/₄ cup) chicken stock

3 dried juniper berries, lightly crushed

2 teaspoons finely chopped rosemary

3 teaspoons finely chopped thyme

3 kg (6 lb 12 oz) turkey, neck and giblets removed

1 large red onion, cut into 4–5 slices

30 g (1 oz) butter, softened

375 ml (13 fl oz/1¹/₂ cups) dry white wine

1 carrot, quartered

1 celery stalk, quartered

1 large rosemary sprig

2 teaspoons finely chopped thyme

250 ml (9 fl oz/1 cup) chicken stock

2 tablespoons plain (all-purpose) flour

SERVES 6–8

Preheat the oven to 170°C (325°F/Gas 3). Soak the prunes in hot water for 20 minutes. Meanwhile, to prepare the chestnuts, make a small cut in the skin on the flat side, put under a hot grill (broiler) and cook on both sides until well browned. Put the hot chestnuts in a bowl lined with a damp tea towel (dish towel) and cover with the towel. Leave until cool enough to handle, then peel. Do not allow the chestnuts to cool completely before peeling, as they will become harder to peel as they cool. Roughly chop the prunes and chestnuts and set aside.

To make the stuffing, melt the butter in a large saucepan and add the onion, garlic and pancetta. Cook over low heat for 5–6 minutes, or until the onion is softened but not brown. Add the rice, stock, juniper berries, prunes and chestnuts, stir well, then pour in 375 ml (13 fl oz/1¹/₂ cups) water. Bring to the boil and cook, covered, stirring once or twice, for 20–25 minutes, or until the rice is tender and all liquid has been absorbed. Remove from the heat, stir in the rosemary and thyme, and season.

Wash and thoroughly pat dry the turkey. Fill the turkey cavity with the stuffing. Cross the turkey legs and tie them together, then tuck the wings underneath the body. Arrange the onion slices in the centre of a large roasting tin, then sit the turkey on top, breast side up. Season and dot with butter. Pour 250 ml (9 fl oz/1 cup) of the wine into the tin, then scatter the carrot, celery, rosemary and 1 teaspoon of the thyme around the turkey.

Roast for 2–2¹/₂ hours, or until cooked through and the juices run clear, basting every 30 minutes. After 1 hour, pour half the chicken stock into the tin. Once the skin becomes golden brown, cover with buttered foil.

When cooked, transfer the turkey to a carving plate, cover with foil and leave to rest in a warm spot. Meanwhile, pour the juices into a small saucepan and reduce for 8–10 minutes. Stir in the flour, then add the stock, a little at a time, stirring to form a paste. Slowly add the rest of the stock and wine, stirring so that no lumps form. Stir in the remaining thyme. Bring to the boil and continue to simmer for 6–8 minutes, or until reduced by one-third, then season to taste. Transfer to a gravy boat. Carve the turkey and serve with the stuffing and gravy.

PREPARATION TIME: 30 MINUTES +   COOKING TIME: 3 HOURS 30 MINUTES

LAMB TAGINE WITH QUINCE

1.5 kg (3 lb 5 oz) lamb shoulder, cut into
3 cm (1¼ inch) pieces
2 large onions, diced
½ teaspoon ground ginger
½ teaspoon cayenne pepper
¼ teaspoon crushed saffron threads
1 teaspoon ground coriander
1 cinnamon stick
25 g (1 oz) roughly chopped coriander
(cilantro) leaves
40 g (1½ oz) butter
500 g (1 lb 2 oz) quinces, peeled, cored
and quartered
100 g (3½ oz) dried apricots
coriander (cilantro) sprigs, extra,
to garnish

SERVES 4–6

Place the lamb in a heavy-based, flameproof casserole dish and add half the onion, the ginger, cayenne pepper, saffron, ground coriander, cinnamon stick, coriander leaves and some salt and pepper. Cover with cold water and bring to the boil over medium heat. Reduce the heat and simmer, partly covered, for 1½ hours, or until the lamb is tender.

While the lamb is cooking, melt the butter in a heavy-based frying pan and cook the remaining onion and the quinces for 15 minutes over medium heat, or until lightly golden.

When the lamb has been cooking for 1 hour, add the quinces and apricots and continue cooking.

Taste the sauce and adjust the seasoning if necessary. Transfer to a warm serving dish and sprinkle with coriander sprigs. Serve with couscous or rice.

PREPARATION TIME: 20 MINUTES   COOKING TIME: 1 HOUR 40 MINUTES

PORK AND CORIANDER STEW

1½ tablespoons coriander seeds
800 g (1 lb 12 oz) pork fillet, cut
into 2 cm (¾ inch) dice
1 tablespoon plain (all-purpose) flour
60 ml (2 fl oz/¼ cup) olive oil
1 large onion, thinly sliced
375 ml (13 fl oz/1½ cups) red wine
250 ml (9 fl oz/1 cup) chicken stock
1 teaspoon sugar
coriander (cilantro) sprigs, to garnish

SERVES 4–6

Crush the coriander seeds using a mortar and pestle. Transfer to a bowl, add ½ teaspoon cracked black pepper and the pork and toss to coat. Cover and refrigerate overnight.

Add the flour to the pork and toss. Heat 2 tablespoons of the oil in a frying pan and cook the pork in batches over high heat for 1–2 minutes, or until brown. Remove from the pan.

Heat the remaining oil in the pan, add the onion and cook over medium heat for 2–3 minutes, or until just golden. Return the meat to the pan and add the wine, stock and sugar. Season, bring to the boil, then reduce the heat and simmer, covered, for 1 hour.

Remove the meat. Return the pan to the heat and boil over high heat for 3–5 minutes, or until the sauce is reduced and slightly thickened. Pour over the meat and garnish with the coriander sprigs.

PREPARATION TIME: 15 MINUTES +   COOKING TIME: 1 HOUR 20 MINUTES

Lamb tagine with quince

MEXICAN BEEF CHILLI WITH BEANS AND RICE

400 g (14 oz/2 cups) long-grain white rice
2 tablespoons olive oil
600 g (1 lb 5 oz) chuck steak, cut into
2 cm (3/4 inch) cubes
1 red onion, chopped
3 garlic cloves, crushed
1 long green chilli, finely chopped
2 1/2 teaspoons ground cumin
2 teaspoons ground coriander
1 teaspoon chilli powder
3 teaspoons dried oregano
400 g (14 oz) tinned chopped tomatoes
2 tablespoons tomato paste
(concentrated purée)
750 ml (26 fl oz/3 cups) beef stock
400 g (14 oz) tinned kidney beans,
drained and rinsed
2 tablespoons oregano, chopped
burritos, to serve
sour cream, to serve

Put the rice in a heatproof bowl, add enough boiling water to cover it and leave it to soak until cool.

Meanwhile, heat 1 tablespoon of the oil in a large, heavy-based saucepan. Cook the beef in two batches until browned, then remove from the pan.

Heat the remaining oil in the pan and cook the onion for 2 minutes, or until softened but not browned. Add the garlic and chilli and cook for a further minute, then add the cumin, coriander, chilli powder and dried oregano and cook for a further 30 seconds. Return the beef to the pan and add the chopped tomatoes, tomato paste and 250 ml (9 fl oz/1 cup) of the stock. Bring to the boil, then reduce the heat and simmer, covered, for 1 1/2 hours, or until the beef is tender.

Drain the rice and stir it into the beef mixture along with the kidney beans and remaining stock. Bring the mixture to the boil, then reduce the heat and simmer, covered, for 20 minutes, or until the rice is tender and all the liquid has been absorbed. Stir in the oregano and serve with warmed burritos and a dollop of sour cream. Let your guests assemble their own burritos at the table.

SERVES 4–6   PREPARATION TIME: 20 MINUTES +   COOKING TIME: 2 HOURS

BREAM WITH TOMATO CHEESE CRUST

2 ripe tomatoes
1 small onion, finely chopped
1 tablespoon tomato paste (concentrated purée)
½ teaspoon ground cumin
½ teaspoon ground coriander
Tabasco sauce, to taste
¼ teaspoon ground pepper
1 tablespoon lemon juice
20 g (¾ oz) butter, melted
4 skinless bream fillets
90 g (3 oz/¾ cup) grated cheddar cheese
40 g (1½ oz/½ cup) fresh breadcrumbs
lemon wedges, to serve

SERVES 4

Score a cross in the base of each tomato. Put in a heatproof bowl and cover with boiling water. Leave for 30 seconds, then transfer to cold water and peel the skin away from the cross. Cut each tomato in half, scoop out the seeds and finely chop the flesh.

Preheat the oven to 180°C (350°F/Gas 4). Lightly grease a baking tray. Put the tomato in a small bowl and mix with the onion, tomato paste, cumin, coriander and Tabasco.

Combine the pepper, lemon juice and butter in a small bowl. Put the bream fillets on the prepared tray. Brush each fillet with the pepper mixture and top with the tomato mixture. Sprinkle with the combined cheddar and breadcrumbs and bake for 15 minutes, or until the fish is tender and flakes easily when tested with a fork. Serve with the lemon wedges.

PREPARATION TIME: 40 MINUTES   COOKING TIME: 15 MINUTES

BRAISED LAMB SHANKS WITH HARICOT BEANS

400 g (14 oz/2 cups) dried haricot beans
80 ml (2½ fl oz/⅓ cup) oil
4 lamb shanks, trimmed
40 g (1½ oz) butter
2 garlic cloves, crushed
2 onions, finely chopped
1½ tablespoons thyme
2 tablespoons tomato paste (concentrated purée)
800 g (1 lb 12 oz) tinned crushed tomatoes
1 tablespoon paprika
1 dried jalapeño chilli, roughly chopped
30 g (1 oz) roughly chopped flat-leaf (Italian) parsley

SERVES 4

Put the beans in a bowl, cover with water and soak overnight. In a large heavy-based saucepan, heat 3 tablespoons of the oil over medium heat and brown the lamb on all sides. Remove, then set aside and drain the fat from the pan. Heat the butter and remaining oil in the pan and cook the garlic and onion over medium heat for 3–4 minutes, or until softened. Add the thyme, tomato paste, tomatoes and paprika and simmer for 5 minutes. Add the lamb shanks and 500 ml (17 fl oz/2 cups) hot water. Season and bring to the boil. Cover, reduce the heat and simmer gently for 30 minutes.

Drain the beans and add to the pan with the chilli and another 500 ml (17 fl oz/2 cups) hot water. Bring to the boil again, cover and simmer for another 1–1½ hours, or until the beans and the meat are tender, adding more water, 125 ml (4 fl oz/½ cup) at a time, if necessary. Adjust the seasoning if necessary and stir in half the parsley. Serve hot, sprinkled with the remaining parsley.

PREPARATION TIME: 10 MINUTES +   COOKING TIME: 2 HOURS 15 MINUTES

SEAFOOD, FENNEL AND POTATO STEW

18–20 black mussels
6 baby octopus
16 raw prawns (shrimp)
1 large fennel bulb
2 tablespoons olive oil
2 leeks, white part only, thinly sliced
2 garlic cloves, crushed
$\frac{1}{2}$ teaspoon paprika
2 tablespoons Pernod or Ricard
(see Notes)
170 ml ($5\frac{1}{2}$ fl oz/$\frac{2}{3}$ cup) dry white wine
$\frac{1}{4}$ teaspoon saffron threads
$\frac{1}{4}$ teaspoon thyme
500 g (1 lb 2 oz) fish cutlets (such as
swordfish, kingfish, warehou, monkfish),
cut into 6 large chunks
400 g (14 oz) small boiling potatoes
(see Notes)

SERVES 6

Scrub the mussels with a stiff brush and pull out the hairy beards. Discard any broken mussels or open ones that don't close when tapped on the bench. Rinse well.

Use a small, sharp knife to cut off the octopus heads. Grasp the bodies and push the beaks out with your index finger. Remove and discard. Slit the heads and remove the gut, then wash well.

Peel the prawns, leaving the tails intact. Gently pull out the dark vein from each prawn back, starting at the head end.

Remove the fennel fronds and reserve. Trim off any discoloured parts of the fennel and thinly slice. Heat the oil in a large frying pan over medium heat. Add the fennel, leek and garlic. Stir in the paprika, season lightly and cook for 8 minutes, or until softened. Add the Pernod or Ricard and wine and boil for 1 minute, or until reduced by a third.

Add the mussels to the pan, cover and cook, shaking the pan occasionally for 4–5 minutes, discarding any mussels that haven't opened after that time. Remove from the pan and allow to cool. Remove the mussel meat from the shells and set aside.

Add the saffron and thyme to the pan and cook, stirring over medium heat, for 1–2 minutes. Season if necessary, then transfer to a large, flameproof casserole dish.

Stir the octopus, prawns, fish and potatoes into the stew. Cover and cook gently for 10 minutes, or until the potatoes and seafood are tender. Add the mussels, cover and heat through. Garnish with the reserved fennel fronds and serve.

PREPARATION TIME: 25 MINUTES   COOKING TIME: 30 MINUTES

NOTES: Pernod and Ricard are aniseed-flavoured liqueurs and complement the fennel.

Choose very small potatoes for this recipe. Otherwise, cut larger ones in half.

143

STEAK AND KIDNEY PIE

750 g (1 lb 10 oz) round steak, trimmed of
excess fat and sinew
4 lamb kidneys
2 tablespoons plain (all-purpose) flour
1 tablespoon oil
1 onion, chopped
30 g (1 oz) butter
1 tablespoon worcestershire sauce
1 tablespoon tomato paste
(concentrated purée)
125 ml (4 fl oz/½ cup) red wine
250 ml (9 fl oz/1 cup) beef stock
125 g (4½ oz) button mushrooms, sliced
½ teaspoon dried thyme
4 tablespoons chopped flat-leaf
(Italian) parsley
500 g (1 lb 2 oz) block ready-made puff
pastry, thawed
1 egg, lightly beaten

SERVES 6

Cut the steak into 2 cm (¾ inch) cubes. Peel the skin from the kidneys, quarter them and trim away any fat or sinew. Put the flour in a plastic bag with the meat and kidneys and toss gently. Heat the oil in a frying pan, add the onion and fry for 5 minutes, or until soft. Remove from the pan with a slotted spoon. Add the butter to the pan, brown the steak and kidneys in batches and then return the steak, kidneys and onion to the pan.

Add the worcestershire sauce, tomato paste, wine, stock, mushrooms and herbs to the pan. Bring to the boil, reduce the heat and simmer, covered, for 1 hour, or until the meat is tender. Season to taste and allow to cool. Spoon into a 1.5 litre (52 fl oz/6-cup) pie dish.

Preheat the oven to 210°C (415°F/Gas 6-7). Roll the pastry between two sheets of baking paper, to a size 4 cm (1½ inches) larger than the pie dish. Cut thin strips from the edge of the pastry and press onto the rim of the dish, sealing the joins. Place the pastry on the pie, trim the edges and cut two steam holes in the pastry. Decorate the pie with leftover pastry and brush the top with egg. Bake for 35-40 minutes, or until the pastry is golden.

PREPARATION TIME: 20 MINUTES   COOKING TIME: 1 HOUR 50 MINUTES

SHEPHERD'S PIE

25 g (1 oz) butter
2 onions, finely chopped
30 g (1 oz/¼ cup) plain (all-purpose) flour
½ teaspoon dry mustard
375 ml (13 fl oz/1½ cups) chicken stock
750 g (1 lb 10 oz) lean cooked roast lamb,
trimmed of excess fat and
finely chopped
2 tablespoons worcestershire sauce
4 large all-purpose potatoes
125 ml (4 fl oz/½ cup) hot milk
30 g (1 oz) butter

SERVES 6

Lightly grease a 2 litre (70 fl oz/8-cup) casserole dish. Preheat the oven to 210°C (415°F/Gas 6-7). Melt the butter in a large frying pan, add the onion and stir over medium heat for 5-10 minutes, or until golden. Add the flour and mustard to the pan and cook for 1 minute, or until pale and foaming. Remove from the heat and gradually stir in the stock. Return to the heat and stir until the sauce boils and thickens. Reduce the heat and simmer for 2 minutes. Add the meat and sauce to the pan and stir. Season to taste. Remove from the heat and spoon into the casserole dish.

Steam or boil the potatoes for 10-15 minutes, or until just tender. Drain and mash well. Add the milk and butter to the mashed potato, season and mix until smooth and creamy. Spread evenly over the meat and rough up the surface with the back of a spoon. Bake for 40-45 minutes, or until the meat is heated through and the topping is golden.

PREPARATION TIME: 30 MINUTES   COOKING TIME: 1 HOUR 15 MINUTES

Steak and kidney pie

STICKY DATE PUDDING

200 g (7 oz) dates, pitted and chopped
1 teaspoon bicarbonate of soda
(baking soda)
100 g (3 1/2 oz) unsalted butter
170 g (6 oz/3/4 cup) caster (superfine)
sugar
2 eggs, lightly beaten
1 teaspoon natural vanilla extract
185 g (6 1/2 oz/1 1/2 cups) self-raising flour
whipped cream and raspberries, to serve

SAUCE
185 g (6 1/2 oz/1 cup) soft brown sugar
125 ml (4 fl oz/1/2 cup) pouring (whipping)
cream
100 g (3 1/2 oz) unsalted butter

SERVES 6–8

Preheat the oven to 180°C (350°F/Gas 4). Lightly grease a 20 cm (8 inch) square cake tin. Line the base with baking paper. Combine the dates with 250 ml (9 fl oz/1 cup) water in a small saucepan. Bring to the boil and remove from the heat. Stir in the bicarbonate of soda and set aside to cool to room temperature.

Using electric beaters, beat the butter and sugar in a small bowl until light and creamy. Add the eggs gradually, beating thoroughly after each addition. Add the vanilla and beat until combined. Transfer to a large bowl.

Using a metal spoon, fold in the flour and dates with the liquid and stir until just combined — do not overbeat. Pour into the prepared tin and bake for 50 minutes, until a skewer comes out clean when inserted into the centre of the pudding. Leave in the tin for 10 minutes before turning out.

To make the sauce, combine the sugar, cream and butter in a small saucepan. Stir until the butter melts and the sugar dissolves. Bring to the boil, reduce the heat and simmer for 2 minutes. Pour over slices of pudding and serve immediately, with extra cream and raspberries (if desired).

PREPARATION TIME: 35 MINUTES +   COOKING TIME: 55 MINUTES

147

PEARS POACHED IN WINE

4 firm pears
750 ml (26 fl oz/3 cups) good-quality
red wine
175 g (6 oz/^{3}/$_4$ cup) caster
(superfine) sugar
1 cinnamon stick
60 ml (2 fl oz/^{1}/$_4$ cup) orange juice
5 cm (2 inch) piece orange peel
200 g (7 oz) mascarpone cheese, to serve

SERVES 4

Peel the pears, being careful to keep the pears whole with the stalks still attached.

Put the wine, sugar, cinnamon stick, orange juice and peel in a saucepan that is large enough for the pears to stand upright. Stir over medium heat until the sugar is dissolved. Add the pears to the saucepan and stir gently to coat. The pears should be almost covered with the wine mixture. Cover the pan and simmer for 20–25 minutes, or until the pears are cooked. Allow to cool in the syrup.

Remove the pears with a slotted spoon. Bring the liquid to the boil and boil rapidly until about 185 ml (6 fl oz/^{3}/$_4$ cup) of liquid remains. Serve the pears with a little syrup and some mascarpone.

PREPARATION TIME: 20 MINUTES +   COOKING TIME: 45 MINUTES

CHOCOLATE RICE PUDDING

220 g (7^3/$_4$ oz/1 cup) medium-grain
white rice
500 ml (17 fl oz/2 cups) boiling water
750 ml (26 fl oz/3 cups) milk
125 g (4^1/$_2$ oz) good-quality dark chocolate,
chopped into small pieces
2–3 tablespoons coffee liqueur
(such as Kahlúa)
1–2 tablespoons caster (superfine) sugar
thick (double/heavy) cream, to serve

SERVES 6

Put the rice in a saucepan, add the boiling water and stir until well combined. Boil, stirring occasionally, for 5 minutes, or until the water is nearly absorbed. Add the milk and bring to the boil. Reduce the heat and simmer, covered, over very low heat for 20 minutes, or until the rice is cooked and the pudding is thick and creamy. Do not let the pudding bubble over.

Add the chocolate and coffee liqueur, and stir until the chocolate is melted and well combined. Add the caster sugar, to taste. Spoon into six bowls and serve with the cream.

PREPARATION TIME: 10 MINUTES   COOKING TIME: 30 MINUTES

Pears poached in wine

RHUBARB CRUMBLE

1 kg (2 lb 4 oz) rhubarb
140 g (5 oz/^{2}/$_3$ cup) sugar
100 g (3^1/$_2$ oz) unsalted butter
90 g (3^1/$_4$ oz/^{3}/$_4$ cup) plain (all-purpose) flour
75 g (2^3/$_4$ oz/^{1}/$_3$ cup) raw (demerara) sugar
10 amaretti biscuits (cookies), crushed

CRUNCHY MAPLE CREAM
200 ml (7 fl oz) thick (double/heavy) cream
2 tablespoons golden syrup or pure maple syrup
3 amaretti biscuits (cookies), crushed

SERVES 4–6

Preheat the oven to 200°C (400°F/Gas 6). Trim the rhubarb, cut into short lengths and put in a saucepan with the sugar. Stir over low heat until the sugar has dissolved, then cover and simmer for 8–10 minutes, or until the rhubarb is soft but still chunky. Spoon into a deep 1.5 litre (52 fl oz/6-cup) ovenproof dish.

Rub the butter into the flour until the mixture resembles fine breadcrumbs, then stir in the demerara sugar and biscuits.

Sprinkle the crumble over the stewed rhubarb and bake for 15 minutes, or until the topping is golden brown.

To make the crunchy maple cream, place the cream in a bowl, carefully swirl the golden syrup through, then the crushed biscuits. Do not overmix — there should be rich veins of the crunchy syrup through the cream. Serve with the crumble.

PREPARATION TIME: 15 MINUTES   COOKING TIME: 25 MINUTES

NOTE: Taste the rhubarb, as you may need to add a little more sugar.

MEDITERRANEAN MOOD

153

AÏOLI WITH CRUDITÉS

AÏOLI
4 garlic cloves, crushed
2 egg yolks
310 ml (10³/₄ fl oz/1¹/₄ cups) light olive oil
or vegetable oil
1 tablespoon lemon juice
pinch ground white pepper

12 asparagus spears, woody ends
trimmed
12 radishes, trimmed
¹/₂ telegraph (long) cucumber, seeded,
halved lengthways and cut into batons
1 head of witlof (chicory/Belgian endive),
leaves separated

SERVES 4

To make the aïoli, put the garlic, egg yolks and a pinch of salt in a food processor and process for 10 seconds. With the motor running, add the oil in a thin, slow stream. The mixture will start to thicken. When this happens you can add the oil a little faster. Process until all the oil is incorporated and the aïoli is thick and creamy. Stir in the lemon juice and pepper.

Bring a saucepan of water to the boil, add the asparagus and cook for 1 minute. Remove and plunge into a bowl of iced water.

Arrange the asparagus, radish, cucumber and witlof decoratively on a platter and put the aïoli in a bowl on the platter.

PREPARATION TIME: 15 MINUTES   COOKING TIME: 2 MINUTES

NOTE: It is important that all the ingredients for the aïoli are at room temperature when you start. Should the aïoli start to curdle, beat in 1–2 teaspoons boiling water. If this fails, put another egg yolk in a clean bowl and very slowly whisk into the curdled mixture, one drop at a time, then continue as above.

BAGNA CAÔDA

310 ml (10³/₄ fl oz/1¹/₄ cups) pouring
(whipping) cream
45 g (1³/₄ oz) tinned anchovy fillets,
drained
10 g (¹/₄ oz) butter
2 garlic cloves, crushed

MAKES ABOUT 250 ML (9 FL OZ/1 CUP)

Bring the cream slowly to the boil in a small heavy-based saucepan. Boil for 8 minutes, stirring frequently and taking care that the cream doesn't boil over. This cooking time reduces and thickens the cream.

Meanwhile, finely chop the anchovies. Melt the butter in a small saucepan, add the anchovies and garlic and cook, stirring, over low heat for 1 minute without allowing to brown.

Pour in the cream and mix thoroughly, then season to taste, if necessary. Pour into a serving bowl. Serve warm as a dipping sauce with vegetable crudités. The mixture will thicken on standing.

PREPARATION TIME: 5 MINUTES   COOKING TIME: 8 MINUTES

Aïoli with crudités

SCALLOPS PROVENÇALE

20 scallops, on the shell
600 g (1 lb 5 oz) tomatoes
60 ml (2 fl oz/¼ cup) olive oil
1 onion, finely chopped
4 French shallots, finely chopped
60 ml (2 fl oz/¼ cup) dry white wine
60 g (2¼ oz) butter
4 garlic cloves, crushed
2 tablespoons finely chopped flat-leaf
(Italian) parsley
½ teaspoon thyme
2 tablespoons fresh breadcrumbs

SERVES 4

Take the scallops off their shells. Rinse and reserve the shells. If the scallops need to be cut off, use a small, sharp knife to slice them free, being careful to leave as little meat on the shell as possible. Slice or pull off any vein, membrane or hard white muscle, leaving any roe attached.

Score a cross in the base of each tomato. Put the tomatoes in a heatproof bowl and cover with boiling water. Leave for 30 seconds, then transfer to cold water and peel the skin away from the cross. Cut each tomato in half, scoop out the seeds and finely dice the flesh.

Heat 2 tablespoons of the oil in a frying pan over medium heat until hot, add the onion and shallots, then reduce the heat to low and cook slowly for 5 minutes, or until soft. Add the wine and simmer for several minutes until reduced slightly, then add the tomato. Season and cook, stirring occasionally, for 20 minutes, or until thick and pulpy. Preheat the oven to 180°F (350°F/Gas 4).

Heat the butter and remaining oil in a frying pan over high heat until foamy. Cook half the scallops for 1–2 minutes each side, or until lightly golden. Remove and repeat with the remaining scallops. Set aside.

Add the garlic to the hot scallop pan and stir for 1 minute. Remove from the heat and stir in the parsley, thyme and breadcrumbs.

To serve, warm the shells on a baking tray in the oven. Put a small amount of tomato mixture on each shell, top with a scallop and sprinkle with the breadcrumb and parsley mixture.

PREPARATION TIME: 20 MINUTES   COOKING TIME: 30 MINUTES

SNAILS WITH GARLIC AND HERB BUTTER

400 g (14 oz) tinned snails
125 g (4¹/₂ oz) butter, softened
4 garlic cloves, crushed
2 tablespoons chopped flat-leaf
(Italian) parsley
2 teaspoons snipped chives
36 snail shells (available from speciality
food stores), or use ovenproof
ramekins or dariole moulds
20 g (³/₄ oz/¹/₄ cup) fresh white
breadcrumbs

SERVES 6

Preheat the oven to 200°C (400°F/Gas 6). Rinse the snails under cold water. Drain well and set aside. In a small bowl, combine the butter, garlic, parsley and chives until smooth. Season. Put a small amount of the butter and a snail in each shell. Seal the shells with the remaining butter and sprinkle with the breadcrumbs.

Place the snails on a baking tray with the open end of the snail facing up so that the butter will not run out of the shell. Bake for 5–6 minutes, or until the butter is bubbling and the breadcrumbs are lightly browned. Serve with crusty baguettes.

PREPARATION TIME: 15 MINUTES   COOKING TIME: 5 MINUTES

BRANDADE DE MORUE

450 g (1 lb) salt cod (this is the dried
weight and is about half a cod)
200 g (7 oz) roasting potatoes,
cut into 3 cm (1¹/₄ inch) chunks
150 ml (5 fl oz) olive oil
250 ml (9 fl oz/1 cup) milk
4 garlic cloves, crushed
2 tablespoons lemon juice
olive oil, extra, to drizzle

SERVES 6

Put the salt cod in a large bowl, cover with cold water and soak for 24 hours, changing the water frequently. Drain the cod and place in a large saucepan of clean water. Bring to the boil over medium heat, reduce the heat and simmer for 30 minutes. Drain, then cool for 15 minutes.

Meanwhile, cook the potatoes in a saucepan of boiling, salted water for 12–15 minutes, or until tender. Drain and keep warm.

Remove the skin from the fish and break the flesh into large flaky pieces, discarding any bones. Put the flesh in a food processor. Using two separate pans, gently warm the oil in one, and the milk and garlic in another.

Start the food processor and, with the motor running, alternately add small amounts of the milk and oil until you have a thick, paste-like mixture. Add the potato and process this in short bursts until combined, being careful not to overwork the mixture once the potato has been added. Transfer to a bowl and gradually add the lemon juice, to taste, and plenty of freshly ground black pepper. Gently lighten the mixture by fluffing it up with a fork. Drizzle with the oil before serving. Serve warm or cold with fried bread.

PREPARATION TIME: 25 MINUTES +   COOKING TIME: 45 MINUTES

Snails with garlic and herb butter

HALOUMI WITH SALAD AND GARLIC BREAD

4 firm tomatoes
1 Lebanese (short) cucumber
140 g (5 oz/4 cups) rocket (arugula)
80 g (2³/4 oz/¹/2 cup) kalamata olives
1 loaf crusty unsliced white bread
100 ml (3¹/2 fl oz) olive oil
1 large garlic clove, halved
400 g (14 oz) haloumi cheese
1 tablespoon lemon juice
1 tablespoon chopped oregano

SERVES 4

Preheat the oven to 180°C (350°F/Gas 4). Heat the grill (broiler) to high.

Cut the tomatoes and cucumber into bite-sized chunks and place in a serving dish with the rocket and olives. Mix well.

Slice the bread into eight 1.5 cm (⁵/8 inch) slices, drizzle 1¹/2 tablespoons of the olive oil over the bread and season. Grill until lightly golden, then rub each slice thoroughly with a cut side of the garlic. Wrap loosely in foil and keep warm in the oven.

Cut the haloumi into eight slices. Heat 2 teaspoons of the oil in a shallow frying pan and fry the haloumi slices for 1–2 minutes each side, or until crisp and golden brown.

Whisk together the lemon juice, oregano and remaining olive oil to make a dressing. Season to taste. Pour half the dressing over the salad and toss well. Arrange the haloumi on top and drizzle with the remaining dressing. Serve immediately with the warm garlic bread.

PREPARATION TIME: 20 MINUTES   COOKING TIME: 5 MINUTES

QUAIL IN VINE LEAVES

12 black grapes, halved
1 tablespoon olive oil
1 garlic clove, crushed
4 large quail
8 fresh or preserved vine leaves
4 prosciutto slices
black grapes, extra, halved, to garnish

SERVES 4

Preheat the oven to 180°C (350°F/Gas 4). Toss the grapes with the oil and crushed garlic. Put six grape halves in the cavity of each quail.

If you are using fresh vine leaves, blanch them for 1 minute in boiling water, then remove the central stem. If using preserved vine leaves, wash them under running water to remove any excess preserving liquid.

Wrap each quail in a piece of prosciutto and place each on top of a vine leaf. Place another vine leaf on top of each quail and wrap into parcels, tying with string to secure. Bake on a baking tray for 20–25 minutes, or until juices run clear when tested with a skewer. Serve garnished with the extra grapes.

PREPARATION TIME: 15 MINUTES   COOKING TIME: 25 MINUTES

FRESH BEETROOT WITH GARLIC SAUCE

1 kg (2 lb 4 oz) fresh beetroot (beets),
including leaves
60 ml (2 fl oz/1/4 cup) extra virgin olive oil
1 tablespoon red wine vinegar

GARLIC SAUCE
250 g (9 oz) roasting potatoes,
cut into 2 cm (3/4 inch) cubes
3 garlic cloves, crushed
ground white pepper, to taste
90 ml (3 fl oz) olive oil
1 tablespoon white vinegar

SERVES 6–8

Cut the stems from the beetroot bulbs, leaving a short piece attached. Trim any tough tops from the leaves, then cut the leaves and stem lengths into halves or thirds and wash. Brush the dirt from the bulbs. Cook the beetroot in boiling, salted water for 30–45 minutes, or until tender. Remove with a slotted spoon and cool slightly.

To make the garlic sauce, bring a large saucepan of water to the boil, add the potato and cook for 10 minutes, or until very soft. Drain thoroughly and mash until quite smooth. Stir the garlic, 1/2 teaspoon salt and the pepper into the potato, then gradually pour in the olive oil, mixing well with a wooden spoon. Stir in the vinegar and season to taste.

Return the beetroot cooking water to the boil, add the leaves and stems, and more water if necessary, and boil for 8 minutes, or until tender. Drain and squeeze the excess water from the leaves using your hands. Wear rubber gloves and peel the skin from the bulbs. Cut the bulbs in half and then into thick slices. Arrange the leaves and sliced bulbs on a serving plate. Combine the oil and vinegar and season to taste. Drizzle over the leaves and bulbs, and serve the garlic sauce on the side.

PREPARATION TIME: 40 MINUTES   COOKING TIME: 1 HOUR

Quail in vine leaves

STUFFED CRAB

4 live crabs (about 750 g/1 lb 10 oz each)
(see Note)
55 g (2 oz/¼ cup) salt
80 ml (2½ fl oz/⅓ cup) olive oil
1 onion, finely chopped
1 garlic clove
125 ml (4 fl oz/½ cup) dry white wine
250 ml (9 fl oz/1 cup) tomato passata
(puréed tomatoes)
¼ teaspoon finely chopped tarragon
2 tablespoons dry breadcrumbs
2 tablespoons chopped flat-leaf
(Italian) parsley
40 g (1½ oz) butter, chopped into small
pieces

SERVES 4

Put the crabs in the freezer for 1 hour to immobilize them. Bring a large saucepan of water to the boil. Add the salt and the crabs. Return to the boil and simmer, uncovered, for 15 minutes. Remove the crabs from the water and cool for 30 minutes. Extract the meat from the legs. Lift the apron — the small flap on the underside of the crab — and prise off the top hard shell, without destroying the top shell, which is needed for serving. Reserve any liquid in a bowl. Remove the soft internal organs and pull off the grey feathery gills. Take out the meat and chop finely with the leg meat. Scoop out all the brown paste from the shells and mix with the chopped meat.

Heat the oil in a frying pan and cook the onion and garlic for 5–6 minutes, or until softened. Stir in the wine and passata. Simmer for 3–4 minutes, then add any reserved crab liquid. Simmer for 3–4 minutes. Add the crabmeat and tarragon, then season. Simmer for about 5 minutes, until thick. Discard the garlic.

Preheat the oven to 210°C (415°F/Gas 6–7). Rinse out and dry the crab shells. Divide the crab mixture among them, levelling the surface. Combine the breadcrumbs and parsley and sprinkle over the top. Dot with the butter. Bake for 6–8 minutes, until the butter melts and the breadcrumbs brown. Serve hot.

PREPARATION TIME: 30 MINUTES +   COOKING TIME: 50 MINUTES

NOTE: The crab traditionally used in this recipe is the centollo or spider crab. Substitute any large-bodied fresh crab, but avoid swimmer or spanner crabs, which do not have enough flesh in them.

GARLIC PRAWNS

1.25 kg (2 lb 12 oz) raw prawns (shrimp)
80 g (2¾ oz) butter, melted
185 ml (6 fl oz/¾ cup) olive oil
8 garlic cloves, crushed
2 spring onions (scallions), thinly sliced

SERVES 4

Preheat the oven to 250°C (500°F/Gas 9). Peel the prawns, leaving the tails intact. Gently pull out the vein from each prawn back, starting at the head end. Cut a slit down the back of each prawn.

Combine the butter and oil and divide among four 500 ml (17 fl oz/2-cup) ovenproof pots. Divide half the crushed garlic among the pots.

Place the pots on a baking tray and heat in the oven for 10 minutes, or until the mixture is bubbling. Divide the prawns and remaining garlic among the pots. Return to the oven for 5 minutes, or until the prawns are cooked. Stir in the spring onion. Season to taste. Serve with bread to mop up the juices.

PREPARATION TIME: 20 MINUTES   COOKING TIME: 15 MINUTES

NOTE: Garlic prawns can also be made in a cast-iron frying pan in the oven or on the stovetop.

BAKED PRAWNS WITH FETA

300 g (10½ oz) raw large prawns (shrimp)
2 tablespoons olive oil
2 small red onions, finely chopped
1 large garlic clove, crushed
350 g (12 oz) tomatoes, diced
2 tablespoons lemon juice
2 tablespoons fresh oregano or
1 teaspoon dried
200 g (7 oz) feta cheese
extra virgin olive oil, for drizzling
chopped flat-leaf (Italian) parsley,
to garnish

SERVES 4

Peel the prawns, leaving the tails intact. Gently pull out the dark vein from each prawn back, starting at the head end.

Preheat the oven to 180°C (350°F/Gas 4). Heat the oil in a saucepan over medium heat, add the onion and cook, stirring occasionally for 3 minutes, or until softened. Add the garlic and cook for a few seconds, then add the tomato and cook for 10 minutes, or until the mixture is slightly reduced and thickened. Add the lemon juice and oregano. Season to taste.

Pour half the sauce into a 750 ml (26 fl oz/3-cup) ovenproof dish, about 15 cm (6 inches) square. Place the prawns on top. Spoon on the remaining sauce, then crumble the feta over the top. Drizzle with the extra virgin olive oil and sprinkle with freshly cracked black pepper.

Bake for 15 minutes, or until the prawns are just cooked. Garnish with the parsley and serve immediately with lightly toasted bread to soak up the juices.

PREPARATION TIME: 20 MINUTES   COOKING TIME: 30 MINUTES

Garlic prawns

MOULES MARINIÈRE

26 black mussels
3 onions, chopped
1 celery stalk, chopped
250 ml (9 fl oz/1 cup) dry white wine
375 ml (13 fl oz/1½ cups) fish stock
4 flat-leaf (Italian) parsley sprigs
1 thyme sprig
1 bay leaf
60 g (2¼ oz) butter
2 garlic cloves, crushed
1 teaspoon plain (all-purpose) flour
dill sprigs, to garnish

SERVES 4

Scrub the mussels with a stiff brush and pull out the hairy beards. Discard any broken mussels, or open ones that don't close when tapped on the bench. Rinse well.

Put the mussels, celery, wine and one-third of the onion in a large saucepan and bring rapidly to the boil. Cover and cook, shaking the pan frequently, for 4-5 minutes, discarding any unopened mussels after that time.

Pull off and discard the empty side of each shell. Set aside the mussels in the shells, cover and keep warm.

Strain and reserve the cooking liquid, discarding the vegetables.

In a saucepan, heat the fish stock, parsley, thyme and bay leaf. Bring to the boil, then reduce the heat, cover and simmer for 10 minutes. Remove the herbs.

Melt the butter in a large saucepan, add the garlic and remaining onion and stir over low heat for 5-10 minutes, or until the onion is soft but not brown. Stir in the flour and cook for 1 minute, or until pale and foaming. Remove from the heat and gradually stir in the reserved mussel liquid and fish stock. Return to the heat and stir until the mixture boils and thickens. Reduce the heat and simmer, uncovered, for 10 minutes.

Divide the reserved mussels among four soup bowls. Ladle liquid over the mussels and garnish with the dill sprigs. Serve immediately with slices of fresh crusty bread.

PREPARATION TIME: 15 MINUTES   COOKING TIME: 35 MINUTES

SALAD NIÇOISE

3 eggs
2 vine-ripened tomatoes
175 g (6 oz) baby green beans, trimmed
125 ml (4 fl oz/½ cup) olive oil
2 tablespoons white wine vinegar
1 large garlic clove, halved
325 g (11½ oz) iceberg lettuce heart
1 small red capsicum (pepper)
1 Lebanese (short) cucumber
1 celery stalk
¼ large red onion, thinly sliced
375 g (13 oz) tinned tuna, drained and broken into chunks
12 kalamata olives
45 g (1½ oz) tinned anchovy fillets, drained
2 teaspoons baby capers, rinsed and squeezed dry
12 small basil leaves

SERVES 4

Put the eggs in a saucepan of cold water. Bring to the boil, then reduce the heat and simmer for 10 minutes. Stir during the first few minutes to centre the yolks. Cool under cold water, then peel and cut into quarters. Meanwhile, score a cross in the base of each tomato. Put in a heatproof bowl and cover with boiling water. Leave for 30 seconds, then transfer to cold water and peel the skin away from the cross. Cut each tomato into eight pieces.

Cook the beans in a saucepan of boiling water for 2 minutes, rinse under cold water, then drain.

To make the dressing, whisk together the oil and vinegar.

Rub the garlic over the base and sides of a platter. Cut the lettuce into eight wedges and arrange over the base. Remove the seeds and membrane from the capsicum and thinly slice. Cut the cucumber and celery into thin 5 cm (2 inch) lengths. Layer the egg, tomato, beans, red capsicum, cucumber and celery over the lettuce. Scatter the onion and tuna over them, then the olives, anchovies, capers and basil. Drizzle with dressing and serve.

PREPARATION TIME: 30 MINUTES   COOKING TIME: 15 MINUTES

GREEK SALAD

1 telegraph (long) cucumber, peeled
2 green capsicums (peppers)
4 vine-ripened tomatoes, cut into wedges
1 red onion, thinly sliced
16 kalamata olives
250 g (9 oz) Greek feta, cubed
24 flat-leaf (Italian) parsley leaves
12 mint leaves
125 ml (4 fl oz/½ cup) extra virgin olive oil
2 tablespoons lemon juice
1 garlic clove, crushed

SERVES 4

Cut the cucumber in half lengthways and discard the seeds. Cut into bite-sized pieces. Cut each capsicum in half lengthways, remove the seeds and membrane and cut the flesh into 1 cm (½ inch) wide strips. Gently mix the cucumber, green capsicum, tomato, onion, olives, feta, parsley and mint leaves in a large salad bowl.

To make the dressing, whisk together the oil, lemon juice and garlic, then season. Pour over the salad and serve.

PREPARATION TIME: 20 MINUTES   COOKING TIME: NIL

Salad Niçoise

VEGETABLE TIAN

1 kg (2 lb 4 oz) red capsicums (peppers)
125 ml (4 fl oz/½ cup) olive oil
800 g (1 lb 12 oz) silverbeet (Swiss chard),
stalks removed and roughly shredded
2 tablespoons pine nuts
freshly grated nutmeg, to taste
1 onion, chopped
2 garlic cloves
2 teaspoons chopped thyme
750 g (1 lb 10 oz) tomatoes, peeled,
seeded and diced
1 large eggplant (aubergine), cut into 1 cm
(½ inch) rounds
5 small zucchini (courgettes) (about
500 g/1 lb 2 oz), thinly sliced diagonally
3 tomatoes, cut into 1 cm (½ inch) slices
1 tablespoon fresh breadcrumbs
30 g (1 oz) parmesan cheese, grated
30 g (1 oz) butter

SERVES 6–8

Preheat the oven to 200°C (400°F/Gas 6). Preheat the grill (broiler) to high.

Remove the seeds and membrane from the capsicums and grill (broil), skin side up, until they are black and blistered. Cool in a plastic bag, then peel and cut into 3 x 8 cm (1¼ x 3¼ inch) slices. Place in a lightly greased 5 x 20 x 25 cm (2 x 8 x 10 inch) ovenproof dish and season lightly.

Heat 2 tablespoons of the olive oil in a heavy-based frying pan and cook the silverbeet over medium heat for 8–10 minutes, or until softened. Add the pine nuts and season to taste, with salt, pepper and nutmeg. Place the silverbeet over the capsicum slices.

Heat another tablespoon of olive oil in a heavy-based frying pan. Add the onion and cook over medium heat for 7–8 minutes, or until soft and golden. Add the garlic and thyme, cook for 1 minute, then add the diced tomato and bring to the boil. Reduce the heat and simmer for 10 minutes. Spread the sauce evenly over the silverbeet.

Heat the remaining olive oil in a heavy-based frying pan and fry the eggplant slices over high heat for 8–10 minutes, or until golden on both sides. Drain on paper towels and place in a single layer over the tomato sauce. Season lightly.

Arrange the zucchini and tomato slices in alternating layers over the eggplant. Sprinkle the breadcrumbs and parmesan over the top and then dot with the butter. Bake for 25–30 minutes, or until golden. Serve warm or at room temperature.

PREPARATION TIME: 40 MINUTES   COOKING TIME: 1 HOUR 20 MINUTES

WARM CHICKPEA AND SILVERBEET SALAD WITH SUMAC

250 g (9 oz) dried chickpeas
125 ml (4 fl oz/$\frac{1}{2}$ cup) olive oil
1 onion, cut into thin wedges
2 tomatoes
1 teaspoon sugar
$\frac{1}{4}$ teaspoon ground cinnamon
2 garlic cloves, chopped
1.5 kg (3 lb 5 oz) silverbeet (Swiss chard)
3 tablespoons chopped mint
2–3 tablespoons lemon juice
1$\frac{1}{2}$ tablespoons ground sumac

SERVES 4

Put the chickpeas in a large bowl, cover with water and soak overnight. Drain and put in a large saucepan. Cover with water and bring to the boil, then simmer for 1$\frac{3}{4}$ hours, or until tender. Drain thoroughly.

Heat the oil in a heavy-based frying pan, add the onion and cook over low heat for 5 minutes, or until softened and just starting to brown.

Cut the tomatoes in half, scoop out the seeds and dice the flesh. Add the tomato flesh to the pan with the sugar, cinnamon and garlic, and cook for 2–3 minutes, or until softened.

Thoroughly wash the silverbeet. Pat dry with paper towels. Trim the stems and finely shred the leaves. Add to the tomato mixture with the chickpeas and cook for 3–4 minutes, or until the silverbeet wilts. Add the mint, lemon juice and sumac, season, and cook for 1 minute, then serve.

PREPARATION TIME: 30 MINUTES +   COOKING TIME: 2 HOURS

SPINACH RICE

400 g (14 oz) English spinach
6 spring onions (scallions)
2 tablespoons olive oil
1 large onion, chopped
2 garlic cloves, crushed
330 g (11$\frac{3}{4}$ oz/1$\frac{1}{2}$ cups) short- or medium-grain white rice
2 tablespoons lemon juice
1 tablespoon chopped dill
1 tablespoon chopped flat-leaf (Italian) parsley
375 ml (13 fl oz/1$\frac{1}{2}$ cups) vegetable stock

SERVES 6

Wash the spinach in several changes of water, tear the leaves and chop the stalks. Finely chop the spring onions, including the green tops.

Heat the oil in a large, wide flameproof casserole dish. Add the onion and garlic and cook for 5–7 minutes over medium heat, or until soft. Add the spring onion and rice, stir to coat and cook for 2 minutes, stirring constantly.

Add the spinach, half the lemon juice and the herbs. Season well. Stir in the stock and 375 ml (13 fl oz/1$\frac{1}{2}$ cups) water. Cover, bring to the boil, then reduce the heat to low and cook for 15 minutes.

Remove from the heat and set aside for 5 minutes. Stir in the remaining lemon juice and adjust the seasoning.

PREPARATION TIME: 15 MINUTES   COOKING TIME: 30 MINUTES

Warm chickpea and silverbeet salad with sumac

CHICKEN PIE WITH FETA

1 kg (2 lb 4 oz) boneless, skinless chicken breast

500 ml (17 fl oz/2 cups) chicken stock

60 g (2¼ oz) butter

2 spring onions (scallions), finely chopped

60 g (2¼ oz/½ cup) plain (all-purpose) flour

125 ml (4 fl oz/½ cup) milk

8 sheets filo pastry (30 x 40 cm/ 12 x 16 inches)

60 g (2¼ oz) butter, extra, melted

200 g (7 oz) feta, crumbled

1 tablespoon chopped dill

1 tablespoon snipped chives

¼ teaspoon freshly grated nutmeg

1 egg, lightly beaten

SERVES 6

Cut the chicken into bite-sized pieces. Pour the stock into a saucepan and bring to the boil over high heat. Reduce the heat to low, add the chicken and poach gently for 10–15 minutes, or until the chicken is cooked through. Drain, reserving the stock. Add enough water to the stock in order to bring the quantity up to 500 ml (17 fl oz/2 cups). Preheat the oven to 180°C (350°F/Gas 4).

Melt the butter in a saucepan over low heat, add the spring onion and cook, stirring, for 5 minutes. Add the flour and stir for 30 seconds. Remove the pan from the heat and gradually add the chicken stock and milk, stirring after each addition. Return to the heat and gently bring to the boil, stirring. Simmer for a few minutes, or until the sauce thickens. Remove from the heat.

Line an ovenproof dish measuring 4 x 18 x 25 cm (1½ x 7 x 10 inches) with four sheets of filo pastry, brushing one side of each sheet with melted butter as you go. Place the buttered side down. The filo will overlap the edges of the dish. Cover the unused filo with a damp tea towel (dish towel) to prevent it drying out.

Stir the chicken, feta, dill, chives, nutmeg and egg into the sauce. Season to taste. Pile the mixture on top of the filo pastry in the dish. Fold the overlapping filo over the filling and cover the top of the pie with the remaining four sheets of filo, brushing each sheet with melted butter as you go. Scrunch the edges of the filo so they fit in the dish. Brush the top with butter. Bake for 45–50 minutes, or until the pastry is golden brown and crisp.

PREPARATION TIME: 30 MINUTES   COOKING TIME: 1 HOUR 10 MINUTES

NOTE: If you prefer, you can use puff pastry instead of filo pastry. If you do so, bake in a 220°C (425°F/Gas 7) oven for 15 minutes, then reduce the temperature to 180°C (350°F/Gas 4) and cook for another 30 minutes, or until the pastry is golden.

PORK WITH SAGE AND CAPERS

25 g (1 oz) butter
60 ml (2 fl oz/¼ cup) extra virgin olive oil
1 onion, finely chopped
105 g (3½ oz/1⅓ cups) fresh white breadcrumbs
2 teaspoons chopped sage
1 tablespoon chopped flat-leaf (Italian) parsley
2 teaspoons grated lemon zest
2½ tablespoons salted baby capers, rinsed and drained
1 egg
2 pork fillets (about 500 g/ 1 lb 2 oz each)
8 large, thin bacon or prosciutto slices
2 teaspoons plain (all-purpose) flour
100 ml (3½ fl oz) dry vermouth
310 ml (10¾ fl oz/1¼ cups) chicken or vegetable stock
8 whole sage leaves, extra, to garnish

SERVES 4

Preheat the oven to 170°C (325°F/Gas 3). Heat the butter and 1 tablespoon of the oil in a frying pan, and fry the onion for 5 minutes, or until lightly golden. Mix with the breadcrumbs, sage, parsley, lemon zest, 2 teaspoons of the capers and the egg and season well.

Split each pork fillet in half lengthways and open out. Spread the stuffing down the length of one and cover with the other fillet. Stretch the bacon with the back of a knife and wrap, slightly overlapping around the pork to form a neat parcel. Tie with string. Put in a roasting tin and drizzle with 1 tablespoon of the oil. Bake for 1 hour, or until the juices run clear. Transfer to a carving plate and cover with foil.

Place the roasting tin on the stovetop and stir in the flour. Add the vermouth and allow to bubble for 1 minute. Add the stock and stir to remove any lumps. Simmer for 5 minutes, then add the remaining capers. Heat the remaining oil in a small saucepan and fry the whole sage leaves until crisp. Drain on crumpled paper towels. Carve the pork into 1 cm (½ inch) slices and serve with the sauce and crisp sage leaves.

PREPARATION TIME: 25 MINUTES   COOKING TIME: 1 HOUR 15 MINUTES

DUCK BREAST WITH WALNUT AND POMEGRANATE SAUCE

4 large duck breasts
1 onion, finely chopped
250 ml (9 fl oz/1 cup) fresh pomegranate juice
2 tablespoons lemon juice
2 tablespoons soft brown sugar
1 teaspoon ground cinnamon
185 g (6½ oz/1½ cups) chopped walnuts
pomegranate seeds, to garnish (optional)

SERVES 4

Preheat the oven to 180°C (350°F/Gas 4). Score each duck breast two or three times on the skin side. Cook in a non-stick frying pan over high heat, skin side down, for 6 minutes, or until crisp and most of the fat has been rendered. Put in an ovenproof dish. Remove all but 1 tablespoon of fat from the pan. Add the onion to the pan and cook over medium heat for 2–3 minutes, or until golden. Add the pomegranate juice, lemon juice, sugar, cinnamon and 125 g (4½ oz/1 cup) of the walnuts and cook for 1 minute. Pour over the duck and bake for 15 minutes. Rest the duck for 5 minutes. Skim any excess fat from the sauce. Slice the duck and serve with the sauce. Garnish with the seeds and remaining walnuts.

PREPARATION TIME: 15 MINUTES +   COOKING TIME: 25 MINUTES

Pork with sage and capers

ROAST DUCK WITH OLIVES

SAUCE

2 ripe roma (plum) tomatoes
1 tablespoon olive oil
1 onion, chopped
1 garlic clove, crushed
250 ml (9 fl oz/1 cup) Riesling
2 teaspoons thyme
1 bay leaf
24 niçoise olives, pitted

STUFFING

60 g (2¼ oz/⅓ cup) medium-grain white
rice, cooked
1 garlic clove, crushed
100 g (3½ oz) frozen chopped spinach,
defrosted
2 ducks' livers (about 100 g/3½ oz),
chopped
1 egg, lightly beaten
1 teaspoon thyme

1.8 kg (4 lb) duck
2 bay leaves

SERVES 4

Preheat the oven to 200°C (400°F/Gas 6). Score a cross in the base of each tomato. Put in a heatproof bowl and cover with boiling water. Leave for 30 seconds, then transfer to cold water and peel the skin away from the cross. Cut each tomato in half, scoop out the seeds and finely chop the flesh. To make the sauce, heat the oil in a frying pan, add the onion and cook for 5 minutes, or until transparent. Add the garlic, tomato, wine, herbs and season. Cook for 5 minutes, then add the olives before removing from the heat.

To make the stuffing, thoroughly mix all the ingredients in a bowl and season well. Before stuffing the duck, rinse out the cavity with cold water and pat dry inside and out with paper towels. Put the bay leaves in the cavity, then spoon in the stuffing.

Tuck the wings under the duck, then close the flaps of fat over the parson's nose and secure with a skewer or toothpick. Place in a deep roasting tin and rub 1 teaspoon salt into the skin. Prick the skin all over with a skewer.

Roast on the top shelf of the oven for 35–40 minutes, then carefully pour off the excess fat. Roast for another 35–40 minutes. To check that the duck is cooked, gently pull away one leg from the side. The flesh should be pale brown with no blood in the juices. Carve the duck, then serve with a spoonful of the stuffing and top with the sauce.

PREPARATION TIME: 30 MINUTES   COOKING TIME: 1 HOUR 30 MINUTES

BAKED FISH WITH TOMATO AND ONION

60 ml (2 fl oz/¼ cup) olive oil
2 onions, finely chopped
1 small celery stalk, finely chopped
1 small carrot, finely chopped
2 garlic cloves, chopped
400 g (14 oz) tinned chopped tomatoes
2 tablespoons tomato passata (puréed tomatoes)
¼ teaspoon dried oregano
½ teaspoon sugar
50 g (1¾ oz) white bread, preferably one-day old
500 g (1 lb 2 oz) skinless firm white fish fillets
3 tablespoons chopped flat-leaf (Italian) parsley
1 tablespoon lemon juice

SERVES 4

Preheat the oven to 180°C (350°F/Gas 4). Heat 2 tablespoons of the oil in a heavy-based frying pan. Add the onion, celery and carrot and cook over low heat for 10 minutes, or until soft. Add the garlic, cook for 2 minutes, then add the chopped tomatoes, tomato passata, oregano and sugar. Simmer for about 10 minutes, stirring occasionally, until reduced and thickened. Season.

To make the breadcrumbs, chop the bread in a food processor for a few minutes, until fine crumbs form.

Arrange the fish in a single layer in an ovenproof dish. Stir the chopped parsley and the lemon juice into the sauce. Season to taste, and pour over the fish. Scatter the breadcrumbs all over the top and drizzle with the remaining oil. Bake for 20 minutes, or until the fish is just cooked.

PREPARATION TIME: 20 MINUTES   COOKING TIME: 45 MINUTES

FISH FILLETS WITH HARISSA AND OLIVES

80 ml (2½ fl oz/⅓ cup) olive oil
4 skinless firm white fish fillets
seasoned flour, for dusting
1 onion, chopped
2 garlic cloves, crushed
400 g (14 oz) tinned chopped tomatoes
2 teaspoons harissa
2 bay leaves
1 cinnamon stick
185 g (6½ oz/1 cup) kalamata olives
1 tablespoon lemon juice
2 tablespoons chopped flat-leaf (Italian) parsley

SERVES 4

Heat half the olive oil in a heavy-based frying pan. Dust the fish fillets with flour and cook over medium heat for 2 minutes each side, or until golden. Transfer to a plate.

Add the remaining olive oil to the pan and cook the onion and garlic for 3–4 minutes, or until softened. Add the chopped tomatoes, harissa, bay leaves and cinnamon. Cook for 10 minutes, or until the sauce has thickened. Season to taste.

Return the fish to the pan, add the olives and cover the fish with the sauce. Remove the bay leaves and cinnamon stick and continue cooking for 2 minutes, or until the fish is tender. Add the lemon juice and parsley and serve.

PREPARATION TIME: 15 MINUTES   COOKING TIME: 25 MINUTES

Baked fish with tomato and onion

MOUSSAKA

2 large tomatoes
1.5 kg (3 lb 5 oz) eggplant (aubergine), cut into 5 mm (¼ inch) slices
125 ml (4 fl oz/½ cup) olive oil
2 onions, finely chopped
2 large garlic cloves, crushed
½ teaspoon ground allspice
1 teaspoon ground cinnamon
750 g (1 lb 10 oz) minced (ground) lamb
2 tablespoons tomato paste (concentrated purée)
125 ml (4 fl oz/½ cup) dry white wine
3 tablespoons chopped flat-leaf (Italian) parsley

CHEESE SAUCE
60 g (2¼ oz) butter
60 g (2¼ oz/½ cup) plain (all-purpose) flour
625 ml (21½ fl oz/2½ cups) milk
pinch freshly grated nutmeg
35 g (1¼ oz/⅓ cup) freshly grated kefalotyri or parmesan cheese
2 eggs, lightly beaten

SERVES 6

Score a cross in the base of each tomato. Put in a heatproof bowl and cover with boiling water. Leave for 30 seconds, then transfer to cold water and peel the skin away from the cross. Cut each tomato in half, scoop out the seeds and finely chop the flesh. Lay the eggplant on a tray, sprinkle with salt and leave for 30 minutes. Rinse under water and pat dry.

Heat 2 tablespoons of the olive oil in a frying pan, add the eggplant in batches and cook for 1–2 minutes each side, or until golden and soft. Add a little more oil when needed. Heat 1 tablespoon of the olive oil in a large saucepan, add the onion and cook over medium heat for 5 minutes. Add the garlic, allspice and cinnamon and cook for 30 seconds. Add the lamb and cook for 5 minutes, or until browned, breaking up any lumps with the back of a spoon. Add the tomato, tomato paste and wine, and simmer over low heat for 30 minutes, or until the liquid has evaporated. Stir in the chopped parsley and season to taste. Preheat the oven to 180°C (350°F/Gas 4).

To make the cheese sauce, melt the butter in a saucepan over low heat. Stir in the flour and cook for 1 minute, or until pale and foaming. Remove the saucepan from the heat and gradually stir in the milk and nutmeg. Return the saucepan to the heat and stir constantly until the sauce boils and thickens. Reduce the heat and simmer for 2 minutes. Stir in 1 tablespoon of the cheese until well combined.

Line the base of a 3 litre (104 fl oz/12-cup) ovenproof dish, which measures 25 x 30 cm (10 x 12 inches), with a third of the eggplant. Spoon half the meat sauce over it and cover with another layer of eggplant. Spoon the remaining meat sauce over the top and cover with the remaining eggplant. Stir the egg into the cheese sauce. Spread the sauce over the top of the eggplant and sprinkle with the remaining cheese. Bake for 1 hour. Leave to stand for 10 minutes before slicing.

PREPARATION TIME: 20 MINUTES +   COOKING TIME: 2 HOURS

NOTE: You can substitute an equal quantity of sliced, pan-fried zucchini (courgettes) or potatoes, or any combination of these vegetables for the eggplant.

BEEF PROVENÇALE

1.5 kg (3 lb 5 oz) chuck steak, cut into
3 cm (1¼ inch) cubes
2 tablespoons olive oil
1 small onion, sliced
375 ml (13 fl oz/1½ cups) red wine
2 tablespoons chopped flat-leaf
(Italian) parsley
1 tablespoon chopped rosemary
1 tablespoon chopped thyme
2 bay leaves
250 g (9 oz) speck, rind removed, cut into
1 x 2 cm (½ x ¾ inch) pieces
400 g (14 oz) tinned crushed tomatoes
250 ml (9 fl oz/1 cup) beef stock
500 g (1 lb 2 oz) baby carrots
45 g (1¾ oz/⅓ cup) pitted niçoise olives

SERVES 6

In a bowl, combine the cubed beef with 1 tablespoon of the oil, the onion, 250 ml (9 fl oz/1 cup) of the wine and half the herbs. Cover with plastic wrap and marinate in the refrigerator overnight. Drain the beef, reserving the marinade. Heat the remaining oil in a large heavy-based saucepan and brown the beef and onion in batches. Remove from the pan.

Add the speck to the saucepan and cook for 3–5 minutes, or until crisp. Return the beef to the pan with the remaining wine and marinade and cook, scraping the residue from the base of the pan for 2 minutes, or until the wine has slightly reduced. Add the tomato and stock and bring to the boil. Reduce the heat and add the remaining herbs. Season well, cover and simmer for 1½ hours.

Add the carrots and olives to the saucepan and cook, uncovered, for another 30 minutes, or until the meat and the carrots are tender. Before serving, check the seasoning and adjust if necessary.

PREPARATION TIME: 20 MINUTES +   COOKING TIME: 2 HOURS 25 MINUTES

CHICKEN WITH PRESERVED LEMON AND OLIVES

60 ml (2 fl oz/¼ cup) olive oil
1.6 kg (3 lb 8 oz) chicken
1 onion, chopped
2 garlic cloves, chopped
625 ml (21½ fl oz/2½ cups) chicken stock
½ teaspoon ground ginger
1½ teaspoons ground cinnamon
pinch saffron threads
100 g (3½ oz) green olives
¼ preserved lemon, pulp removed, zest washed and cut into slivers
2 bay leaves
2 chicken livers
3 tablespoons chopped coriander
(cilantro) leaves

SERVES 4

Preheat the oven to 180°C (350°F/Gas 4). Heat 2 tablespoons of the oil in a large frying pan, add the chicken and brown on all sides. Place in a deep flameproof casserole dish. Heat the remaining oil in the pan, add the onion and garlic and cook over medium heat for 3–4 minutes, or until softened. Add the stock, ginger, cinnamon, saffron, olives, lemon and bay leaves and pour around the chicken. Bake for 45 minutes, or until the juices run clear when the thigh is pierced with a skewer, adding a little more water or stock if the sauce gets too dry.

Remove the chicken from the casserole dish, cover with foil and leave to rest. Put the dish on the stovetop over medium heat, add the chicken livers and mash into the sauce as they cook. Cook for 5–6 minutes, or until the sauce has reduced and thickened. Add the chopped coriander. Cut the chicken into four pieces and serve with the sauce.

PREPARATION TIME: 10 MINUTES   COOKING TIME: 1 HOUR

Beef provençale

LAMB BRAISE WITH EGGPLANT CREAM

2 tablespoons olive oil

1 kg (2 lb 4 oz) lamb, cut into 2 cm
(³/4 inch) cubes

1 large onion, chopped

1 bay leaf

small pinch ground cloves

2 garlic cloves, crushed

2 tablespoons tomato paste
(concentrated purée)

400 g (14 oz) tinned chopped tomatoes

30 g (1 oz) chopped flat-leaf
(Italian) parsley

750 ml (26 fl oz/3 cups) beef stock

125 g (4¹/2 oz) vine-ripened tomatoes,
chopped

chopped flat-leaf (Italian) parsley,
to garnish

EGGPLANT CREAM

1 kg (2 lb 4 oz) eggplants (aubergines)

60 g (2¹/4 oz) butter

2¹/2 tablespoons plain (all-purpose) flour

310 ml (10³/4 fl oz/1¹/4 cups) pouring
(whipping) cream

60 g (2¹/4 oz/²/3 cup) grated kasseri
cheese (see Note)

large pinch freshly grated nutmeg

SERVES 6–8

Heat the olive oil in a large, deep saucepan over high heat and cook the lamb in three batches for 4–5 minutes, or until well browned. Remove the lamb from the pan with a slotted spoon and set aside.

Add the onion to the pan, cook for 5 minutes, or until golden, then add the bay leaf, cloves, garlic, tomato paste, tomatoes, parsley, stock and lamb and stir well. Bring to the boil, then reduce the heat to low, cover and simmer, stirring occasionally for 1¹/2 hours, or until the lamb is very tender and the sauce is thick. Season.

Meanwhile, to make the eggplant cream, preheat the oven to 200°C (400°F/Gas 6). Pierce the eggplants a few times with a fork and, using a long-handled fork, roast them over an open flame (either a gas stovetop or a barbecue) for about 5 minutes, turning occasionally, until blackened and blistered all over. This will give them a good smoky flavour. Place the eggplants on a baking tray and bake for about 30 minutes, or until the eggplants are shrivelled and the flesh is very soft. Transfer to a colander and leave to cool.

When cool, peel the eggplants, ensuring all the skin is removed and discarded. Chop the flesh and set aside. Melt the butter in a saucepan over medium heat and add the flour. Stir for 2 minutes, or until it has a toasty aroma and darkens slightly. Gradually pour in the cream, whisking until smooth, then stir in the eggplant. Add the cheese and nutmeg and stir until the cheese has melted. Season.

Spread the eggplant cream on a serving plate, place the lamb in the centre and sprinkle with the chopped tomato and parsley. Serve immediately.

PREPARATION TIME: 30 MINUTES   COOKING TIME: 1 HOUR 45 MINUTES

NOTE: Kasseri cheese, available at specialist delicatessens, is a sheep or goat's milk cheese, often used on top of lamb stews.

CHICKEN WITH FORTY CLOVES OF GARLIC

10 g (¹/₄ oz) butter
1 tablespoon olive oil
1 large chicken
40 garlic cloves, unpeeled
2 tablespoons chopped rosemary
2 thyme sprigs
270 ml (9¹/₂ fl oz) dry white wine
150 ml (5 fl oz) chicken stock
225 g (8 oz/1³/₄ cups) plain (all-purpose) flour

SERVES 4

Preheat the oven to 180°C (350°F/Gas 4). Melt the butter and oil in a 4.5 litre (156 fl oz/18-cup) flameproof casserole dish, then brown the chicken over medium heat until golden all over. Remove the chicken and add the garlic, rosemary and thyme and cook together for 1 minute. Return the chicken to the dish and add the wine and chicken stock. Bring to a simmer, basting the chicken with the sauce.

Put the flour in a bowl and add up to 150 ml (5 fl oz) water to form a pliable paste. Divide into four and roll into cylinder shapes. Place around the rim of the casserole. Put the lid on the dish, pressing down to form a seal. Bake for 1¹/₄ hours. Remove the lid by cracking the paste. Return the chicken to the oven to brown for 15 minutes, then transfer to a plate. Reduce the juices to 250 ml (9 fl oz/1 cup) over medium heat. Carve the chicken, pierce the garlic skins and squeeze the flesh onto the chicken. Serve with the sauce.

PREPARATION TIME: 20 MINUTES   COOKING TIME: 1 HOUR 45 MINUTES

CHICKEN WITH CAPSICUM AND OLIVES

6 tomatoes
1.5 kg (3 lb 5 oz) chicken, cut into 8 portions
60 ml (2 fl oz/¹/₄ cup) olive oil
2 large red onions, sliced into 5 mm (¹/₄ inch) slices
2 garlic cloves, crushed
3 red capsicums (peppers), seeded and membrane removed, cut into 1 cm (¹/₂ inch) strips
60 g (2¹/₂ oz) thickly sliced prosciutto, finely chopped
1 tablespoon chopped thyme
2 teaspoons sweet paprika
8 pitted black olives
8 pitted green olives

SERVES 4

Score a cross in the base of each tomato. Put in a heatproof bowl and cover with boiling water. Leave for 30 seconds, then transfer to cold water and peel the skin away from the cross. Cut each tomato in half, scoop out the seeds and finely chop the flesh. Pat the chicken dry with paper towels and season. Heat the oil in a heavy-based frying pan and cook the chicken a few pieces at a time, skin side down, for 4–5 minutes, until golden. Turn the chicken over and cook for another 2–3 minutes. Transfer to a plate.

Add the onion, garlic, capsicum, prosciutto and thyme to the pan. Cook over medium heat, stirring frequently for 8–10 minutes, or until the vegetables have softened but not browned. Add the tomato and paprika, increase the heat and cook for 10–12 minutes, or until sauce has thickened and reduced. Return the chicken to the pan and coat well with the sauce. Cover the pan, reduce the heat and simmer the chicken for 25–30 minutes, or until tender. Add the olives and adjust the seasoning before serving.

PREPARATION TIME: 30 MINUTES   COOKING TIME: 1 HOUR 10 MINUTES

Chicken with forty cloves of garlic

STUFFED SQUID WITH RICE

8 small squid
about 2 teaspoons plain (all-purpose) flour

STUFFING
1 small onion
2 tablespoons olive oil
2 tablespoons currants
2 tablespoons pine nuts
25 g (1 oz/⅓ cup) fresh breadcrumbs
1 tablespoon chopped mint
1 tablespoon chopped flat-leaf
(Italian) parsley
1 egg, lightly beaten

SAUCE
1 tablespoon olive oil
1 small onion, finely chopped
1 garlic clove, crushed
60 ml (2 fl oz/¼ cup) dry white wine
400 g (14 oz) tinned chopped tomatoes
½ teaspoon sugar
1 bay leaf

RICE
1.25 litres (44 fl oz/5 cups) fish stock
60 ml (2 fl oz/¼ cup) olive oil
1 onion, finely chopped
3 garlic cloves, crushed
275 g (9¾ oz/1¼ cups) calasparra or
short-grain white rice
¼ teaspoon cayenne pepper
3 teaspoons squid ink or four 4 g
sachets
60 ml (2 fl oz/¼ cup) dry white wine
60 g (2¼ oz/¼ cup) tomato paste
(concentrated purée)
2 tablespoons chopped flat-leaf
(Italian) parsley

SERVES 4

To clean the squid, pull each body from the tentacles. Cut off and keep the tentacles as well as the fins from either side of each body sac. If using the ink sacs, extract them and squeeze the ink into a small bowl. Peel the skin from each body sac and dislodge and remove the quills. Rinse under cold water.

To make the stuffing, chop the tentacles, fins and onion in a processor until finely chopped. Heat the oil in a frying pan and cook the currants and pine nuts over low heat, stirring until the nuts are lightly browned. Transfer to a bowl using a slotted spoon. Add the onion mixture to the pan and cook gently over low heat for 5 minutes. Add to the bowl and add the breadcrumbs, mint, parsley and egg. Season and mix well. Stuff into the squid bodies. Close the openings and secure with toothpicks. Dust the squid with the flour.

To make the sauce, wipe out the frying pan with paper towels. Heat the oil, add the onion and cook over low heat for 5 minutes, or until softened. Stir in the garlic, cook for 30 seconds, then add the wine. Cook over high heat for 1 minute, then add the tomato, sugar and bay leaf. Season, reduce the heat and simmer for 5 minutes. Stir in 125 ml (4 fl oz/½ cup) water. Place the squid in the pan in a single layer. Simmer, covered, for about 20 minutes, or until the squid are tender.

To make the rice, bring the stock to a simmer in a saucepan. Heat the oil in a large saucepan, add the onion and cook over low heat for 5 minutes, or until softened. Add the garlic, cook for 15 seconds, then stir in the rice and cayenne pepper. Mix the ink with 80 ml (2½ fl oz/⅓ cup) of hot stock. Stir into the rice, then add the wine and tomato paste. Stir until the liquid has almost all evaporated, then add 250 ml (9 fl oz/1 cup) of the hot stock. Simmer until this evaporates, then stir in more stock, 250 ml (9 fl oz/1 cup) at a time, until the rice is tender and creamy, about 15 minutes. Cover the pan and leave off the heat for 5 minutes. Season well.

To serve, spread the rice on a warm platter and stir in the parsley. Arrange the squid on top and spoon on the sauce.

PREPARATION TIME: 40 MINUTES   COOKING TIME: 1 HOUR 15 MINUTES

SOUVLAKI

1 kg (2 lb 4 oz) boned leg of lamb, trimmed and cut into 2 cm (³/₄ inch) cubes
60 ml (2 fl oz/¹/₄ cup) olive oil
2 teaspoons finely grated lemon zest
80 ml (2¹/₂ fl oz/¹/₃ cup) lemon juice
125 ml (4 fl oz/¹/₂ cup) dry white wine
2 teaspoons dried oregano
2 large garlic cloves, finely chopped
2 bay leaves
250 g (9 oz/1 cup) Greek-style yoghurt
2 garlic cloves, extra, crushed

SERVES 4

If using wooden skewers, soak them for about 30 minutes to prevent them from burning during cooking. Put the lamb in a non-metallic bowl with 2 tablespoons of the oil, the lemon zest and juice, wine, oregano, garlic, bay leaves and some black pepper. Toss, then cover and refrigerate overnight.

Put the yoghurt and extra garlic in a bowl, mix well and leave for 30 minutes.

Drain the lamb. Thread onto eight skewers and cook on a barbecue or chargrill plate, brushing with the remaining oil, for 7–8 minutes, or until done to your liking. Serve with the yoghurt, some bread and a salad.

PREPARATION TIME: 20 MINUTES +   COOKING TIME: 10 MINUTES

SLOW-ROASTED LAMB WITH CUMIN AND PAPRIKA

2.25 kg (5 lb) leg of lamb
80 g (2³/₄ oz) butter, softened
3 garlic cloves, crushed
2 teaspoons ground cumin
3 teaspoons ground coriander
1 teaspoon paprika
1 tablespoon ground cumin, extra, for dipping

SERVES 6

Preheat the oven to 220°C (425°F/Gas 7). With a small sharp knife, cut small deep slits in the top and sides of the lamb.

Mix the butter, garlic, spices and ¹/₄ teaspoon salt in a bowl until a smooth paste forms.

With the back of a spoon, rub the paste all over the lamb, then use your fingers to spread the paste and make sure all the lamb is covered.

Put the lamb, bone side down, in a deep roasting tin and place on the top shelf of the oven. Bake for 10 minutes, then baste and return to the oven. Reduce the temperature to 160°C (315°F/Gas 2–3). Bake for 3 hours 20 minutes, basting every 20–30 minutes. Basting makes the lamb tender and flavoursome. Carve the lamb into chunky slices. Mix the cumin with 1¹/₂ teaspoons salt and serve on the side for dipping.

PREPARATION TIME: 15 MINUTES   COOKING TIME: 3 HOURS 30 MINUTES

SEAFOOD PAELLA

2 tomatoes
500 g (1 lb 2 oz) raw prawns (shrimp)
250 g (9 oz) black mussels
200 g (7 oz) squid rings
60 ml (2 fl oz/¼ cup) olive oil
1 large onion, diced
3 garlic cloves, finely chopped
1 small red capsicum (pepper), seeded
and membrane removed, thinly sliced
1 small red chilli, seeded and chopped
(optional)
2 teaspoons paprika
1 teaspoon ground turmeric
1 tablespoon tomato paste
(concentrated purée)
440 g (15½ oz/2 cups) paella rice
or risotto rice
125 ml (4 fl oz/½ cup) dry white wine
¼ teaspoon saffron threads, soaked in
60 ml (2 fl oz/¼ cup) hot water
1.25 litres (44 fl oz/5 cups) fish stock
300 g (10½ oz) skinless firm white fish
fillets, cut into 2.5 cm (1 inch) cubes
3 tablespoons chopped flat-leaf (Italian)
parsley, to serve
lemon wedges, to serve

SERVES 6

Score a cross in the base of each tomato. Put the tomatoes in a heatproof bowl and cover with boiling water. Leave for 30 seconds, then transfer to cold water and peel the skin away from the cross. Cut each tomato in half, scoop out the seeds and finely chop the flesh.

Peel the prawns, leaving the tails intact. Gently pull out the dark vein from each prawn back, starting at the head end. Scrub the mussels with a stiff brush and pull out the hairy beards. Discard any broken mussels or open ones that don't close when tapped on the bench. Rinse well. Refrigerate the seafood (including the squid), covered, until ready to use.

Heat the oil in a paella pan or large, deep frying pan with a lid. Add the onion, garlic, capsicum and chilli to the pan and cook over medium heat for 2 minutes, or until the onion and capsicum are soft. Add the paprika, turmeric and 1 teaspoon salt and stir-fry for 1–2 minutes, or until fragrant.

Add the chopped tomatoes and cook for 5 minutes, or until softened. Add the tomato paste. Stir in the rice until it is well coated.

Pour in the wine and simmer until almost absorbed. Add the saffron and its soaking liquid and all the fish stock and bring to the boil. Reduce the heat and simmer for 20 minutes, or until almost all the liquid is absorbed into the rice. There is no need to stir the rice, but you may occasionally wish to fluff it up with a fork to separate the grains.

Add the mussels to the pan, poking the shells into the rice, cover and cook for 1–2 minutes over low heat. Add the prawns and cook for 2–3 minutes. Add the fish, cover and cook for 3 minutes. Finally, add the squid rings and cook for 1–2 minutes. By this time, the mussels should have opened — discard any unopened ones. The prawns should be pink and the fish should flake easily when tested with a fork. The squid should be white, moist and tender. Cook for another 2–3 minutes if the seafood is not quite cooked, but avoid overcooking or the seafood will toughen and dry out. Remove the pan from the heat, cover loosely with foil and leave to rest for 5–10 minutes. Serve with the parsley and lemon wedges. Delicious with a tossed salad.

PREPARATION TIME: 25 MINUTES   COOKING TIME: 45 MINUTES

CREMA CATALANA

1 litre (35 fl oz/4 cups) milk
1 vanilla bean
1 cinnamon stick
zest of 1 small lemon, sliced into strips
2 strips orange zest (2 x 4 cm/
$^3/_4$ x 1$^1/_2$ inches)
8 egg yolks
115 g (4 oz/$^1/_2$ cup) caster (superfine)
sugar
40 g (1$^1/_2$ oz/$^1/_3$ cup) cornflour (cornstarch)
45 g (1$^3/_4$ oz/$^1/_4$ cup) soft brown sugar

SERVES 6

Put the milk in a saucepan. Split the vanilla bean lengthways, scrape the seeds into the milk and put the bean in too. Add the cinnamon stick and lemon and orange zest and bring to the boil. Simmer for 5 minutes, then strain and set aside.

Whisk the egg yolks with the caster sugar in a bowl for about 5 minutes, or until pale and creamy. Add the cornflour and mix well. Slowly add the warm milk mixture to the egg and whisk continuously. Return to the pan and cook over medium–low heat, stirring constantly, for 5–10 minutes, or until the mixture is thick and creamy. Do not boil as it will curdle. Pour into six 250 ml (9 fl oz/1-cup) ramekins or dariole moulds and refrigerate for 6 hours, or overnight.

When ready to serve, sprinkle the custards evenly with brown sugar and grill (broil) for 3 minutes, or until the sugar caramelizes.

PREPARATION TIME: 15 MINUTES +   COOKING TIME: 20 MINUTES

SWEET SAFFRON RICE

1 teaspoon saffron threads
2 tablespoons boiling water
110 g (3$^3/_4$ oz/$^1/_2$ cup) medium-grain
white rice
230 g (8$^1/_2$ oz/1 cup) caster (superfine)
sugar
2 tablespoons rosewater
40 g (1$^1/_2$ oz/$^1/_4$ cup) pine nuts, toasted
35 g (1$^1/_4$ oz/$^1/_4$ cup) pistachio nuts,
chopped

SERVES 6

Crush the saffron threads with your fingers and soak in the boiling water for 30 minutes.

Bring 1.25 litres (44 fl oz/5 cups) water to the boil in a large saucepan and add the rice. Reduce to a simmer and cook, stirring occasionally, for 20 minutes. Stir in the caster sugar, rosewater and the saffron with the soaking liquid and simmer for another 10 minutes.

Add the pine nuts and pistachio nuts and simmer for another 10 minutes. The mixture should be thick and soupy. If it is too thick, add a little more water. Serve either hot or cold (it will thicken as it cools), perhaps garnished with pomegranate seeds or pistachio nuts. Serve with Greek-style yoghurt.

PREPARATION TIME: 10 MINUTES +   COOKING TIME: 40 MINUTES

Crema Catalana

BAKLAVA

540 g (1 lb 3 oz/2^1/$_3$ cups) caster (superfine) sugar
1^1/$_2$ teaspoons grated lemon zest
90 g (3^1/$_4$ oz/^{1}/$_4$ cup) honey
60 ml (2 fl oz/^{1}/$_4$ cup) lemon juice
2 tablespoons orange blossom water
200 g (7 oz) walnuts, finely chopped
200 g (7 oz) pistachio nuts, finely chopped
200 g (7 oz) almonds, finely chopped
2 tablespoons caster (superfine) sugar, extra
2 teaspoons ground cinnamon
200 g (7 oz) unsalted butter, melted
375 g (13 oz) filo pastry

MAKES 18 PIECES

Put the sugar, lemon zest and 375 ml (13 fl oz/1^1/$_2$ cups) water in a saucepan and stir over high heat until the sugar has dissolved, then boil for 5 minutes. Reduce the heat to low and simmer for 5 minutes, or until the syrup has thickened slightly and just coats the back of a spoon. Add the honey, lemon juice and orange blossom water and cook for 2 minutes. Remove from the heat and leave to cool completely.

Preheat the oven to 170°C (325°F/Gas 3). Combine the nuts, extra sugar and cinnamon in a bowl. Brush the base and sides of a 27 x 30 cm (10^3/$_4$ x 12 inch) ovenproof dish or tin with the melted butter. Cover the base with a single layer of filo pastry, brush lightly with the butter, folding in any overhanging edges. Continue layering the filo, brushing each new layer with butter and folding in the edges until 10 sheets have been used. Keep the unused filo under a damp tea towel (dish towel).

Sprinkle half the nut mixture over the pastry and pat down evenly. Repeat the layering and buttering of five more filo sheets, sprinkle with the remaining nuts, then continue to layer and butter the remaining sheets, including the top layer. Press down with your hands so the pastry and nuts stick to each other. Using a large sharp knife, cut into diamond shapes, ensuring you cut through to the bottom layer. Pour any remaining butter evenly over the top and smooth with your hands. Bake for 30 minutes, then reduce the temperature to 150°C (300°F/Gas 2) and cook for another 30 minutes.

Immediately cut through the original diamond markings, then strain the syrup evenly over the top. Cool completely before lifting the diamonds out onto a serving platter.

PREPARATION TIME: 30 MINUTES + COOKING TIME: 1 HOUR 15 MINUTES

NOTE: To achieve the right texture, it is important for the baklava to be piping hot and the syrup cold when pouring the syrup.

LAVENDER ICE CREAM

8 stems English lavender (or 4-6 if the
lavender is in full flower, as it has a
stronger flavour)
625 ml (21/2 fl oz/2 1/2 cups) thick
(double/heavy) cream
1 small piece lemon peel
165 g (5 3/4 oz/3/4 cup) sugar
4 egg yolks, lightly whisked

SERVES 6–8

Wash and dry the English lavender, then put it in a saucepan with the cream and lemon peel. Heat until almost boiling, then stir in the sugar until dissolved. Strain through a fine sieve, then gradually pour onto the egg yolks in a bowl, return to the pan and stir over low heat until thick enough to coat the back of a spoon — do not boil. Pour the mixture into a chilled baking dish and set aside to cool slightly, then cover and refrigerate until cold.

Transfer to an ice cream machine and freeze according to manufacturer's instructions. Alternatively, transfer to a shallow metal tray and freeze, whisking every couple of hours until frozen and creamy. Freeze for 5 hours or overnight. Soften in the fridge for 30 minutes before serving.

PREPARATION TIME: 15 MINUTES +   COOKING TIME: 15 MINUTES

FIGS IN HONEY SYRUP

100 g (3 1/2 oz) blanched, whole almonds
12 whole fresh figs (about 750 g/1 lb 10 oz)
110 g (3 3/4 oz/1/2 cup) sugar
115 g (4 oz/1/3 cup) honey
2 tablespoons lemon juice
6 cm (2 1/2 inch) piece lemon peel
1 cinnamon stick
250 g (9 oz/1 cup) Greek-style yoghurt

SERVES 4

Preheat the oven to 180°C (350°F/Gas 4). Place the almonds on a baking tray and bake for 5 minutes, or until golden. Leave to cool. Cut the stems off the figs and make a small crossways incision 5 mm (1/4 inch) deep on top of each. Push a blanched almond into the base of each fig. Roughly chop the remaining almonds.

Put 750 ml (26 fl oz/3 cups) water in a large saucepan, add the sugar and stir over medium heat until the sugar dissolves. Increase the heat and bring to the boil. Stir in the honey, lemon juice, lemon peel and cinnamon stick. Reduce the heat to medium, put the figs in the pan and simmer gently for 30 minutes. Remove with a slotted spoon and place on a large serving dish.

Boil the liquid over high heat for about 15–20 minutes, or until thick and syrupy. Remove the cinnamon and lemon peel. Cool the syrup slightly and pour over the figs. Sprinkle with the chopped almonds. Serve warm or cold with the yoghurt.

PREPARATION TIME: 20 MINUTES   COOKING TIME: 1 HOUR

Lavender ice cream

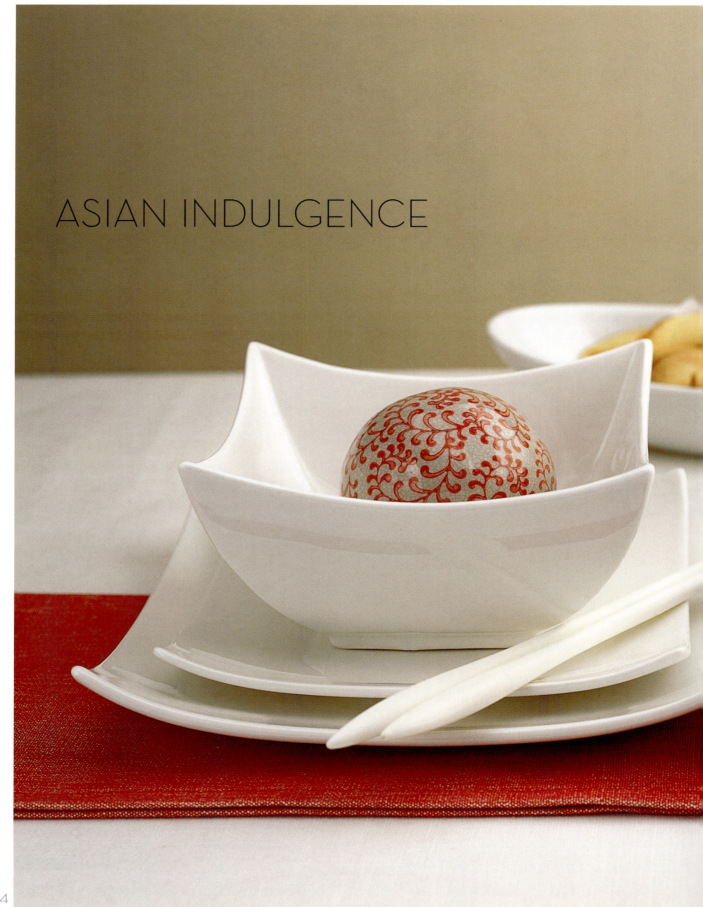

ASIAN INDULGENCE

LAYERED SUSHI

550 g (1 lb 4 oz/2½ cups) Japanese
short-grain rice
1 piece kombu (optional)
100 ml (3½ fl oz) rice vinegar
1 tablespoon mirin
55 g (2 oz/¼ cup) caster (superfine)
sugar
90 g (3¼ oz/⅓ cup) Japanese
mayonnaise (see Note)
2 teaspoons wasabi paste
4 sheets roasted nori
300 g (10½ oz) smoked salmon
40 g (1½ oz/¼ cup) pickled ginger slices,
to garnish
black sesame seeds, to garnish

MAKES 36

Wash the rice in a strainer under cold running water until the water runs clear, then leave in the strainer to drain for an hour. Put the rice and kombu in a saucepan with 750 ml (26 fl oz/3 cups) water and bring to the boil. Cook for 5–10 minutes, or until tunnels form on the surface of the rice, then remove the kombu. Reduce the heat to low, cover and cook the rice for 12–15 minutes, or until the rice is cooked and all the water has been absorbed. Remove from the heat, remove the lid from the pan, cover the rice with a clean tea towel (dish towel) and leave for 15 minutes.

To make the sushi dressing, combine the vinegar, mirin, sugar and 1 teaspoon salt in a small bowl and stir until the sugar has dissolved.

Spread the rice over the base of a non-metallic dish or bowl, pour the dressing over the top and use a spatula or a rice paddle to mix the dressing through the rice, separating the grains — the aim is to make the rice grains stick together slightly. Fan the rice until it cools to room temperature.

Combine the mayonnaise and wasabi in a small bowl. Lay a sheet of nori, shiny side up, on top of a piece of baking paper on a dry tray. Entirely cover the nori with a cup of loosely packed rice. Spread with a little wasabi mayonnaise, then top with a layer of smoked salmon and some slices of pickled ginger. Place another sheet of nori on top and flatten lightly with a rolling pin. Repeat the layering twice, to form three layers, finishing with a sheet of nori, and again flattening with the rolling pin. Reserve the remaining wasabi mayonnaise.

Cover and refrigerate for at least an hour, then, using a very sharp knife dipped in water, trim any filling protruding from the edges and slice into 2 cm (¾ inch) squares. Garnish with wasabi mayonnaise, pickled ginger and black sesame seeds.

PREPARATION TIME: 25 MINUTES +   COOKING TIME: 35 MINUTES

NOTE: Japanese mayonnaise typically comes in easy-to-use squeeze bottles. If you can't find it, use whole-egg mayonnaise instead.

THAI STUFFED MUSSELS

2 kg (4 lb 8 oz) black mussels
125 ml (4 fl oz/$^{1}/_{2}$ cup) dry white wine
3 garlic cloves, chopped
4 coriander (cilantro) roots
1 lemon grass stem
1 lime, sliced
2 small red onions, chopped
1 tablespoon peanut oil
200 g (7 oz/1 cup) jasmine rice
80 g (2$^{3}/_{4}$ oz/$^{1}/_{2}$ cup) roasted unsalted peanuts, chopped
2 teaspoons finely chopped fresh ginger
1 tablespoon fish sauce
1 tablespoon tamarind purée
4 tablespoons coriander (cilantro) leaves, chopped
4 makrut (kaffir lime) leaves, shredded
shredded Vietnamese mint, to garnish

SERVES 6

Scrub the mussels with a stiff brush and remove the hairy beards. Discard any broken mussels or open ones that don't close when tapped on the bench. Rinse well. Put the mussels in a large bamboo steamer and cover.

Put the wine, 375 ml (13 fl oz/1$^{1}/_{2}$ cups) water, two-thirds of the garlic, the coriander roots, the green part of the lemon grass stem, the lime slices and half of the chopped onions in a wok. Bring to a simmer. Sit the steamer over the wok and steam for about 4–5 minutes, or until the mussels open. Discard any unopened mussels. Remove and discard the upper shells. Strain and reserve the cooking liquid.

Heat the oil in a wok over medium heat. Add the remaining onion and garlic, the finely chopped white part of the lemon grass stem and the rice, and stir-fry for 2–3 minutes, or until the onion is soft. Add 500 ml (17 fl oz/2 cups) of the reserved liquid and simmer for 20 minutes. Preheat the oven to 200°C (400°F/Gas 6).

Toss in the peanuts, ginger, fish sauce, tamarind, coriander and makrut (kaffir lime) leaves. Spoon a little of the mixture onto each shell half, transfer to an ovenproof dish and bake for 10 minutes. Garnish with the shredded mint and serve.

PREPARATION TIME: 45 MINUTES   COOKING TIME: 45 MINUTES

CHICKEN WITH NORI

400 g (14 oz) chicken breast tenderloins
60 ml (2 fl oz/$^{1}/_{4}$ cup) Japanese soy sauce
60 ml (2 fl oz/$^{1}/_{4}$ cup) mirin
4 cm (1$^{1}/_{2}$ inches) fresh ginger, very finely grated
1 sheet nori, finely chopped or crumbled into very small pieces
40 g (1$^{1}/_{2}$ oz/$^{1}/_{3}$ cup) cornflour (cornstarch)
250 ml (9 fl oz/1 cup) oil

MAKES 30

Carefully trim and discard any sinew from the chicken, then cut the chicken into bite-sized pieces and put them in a bowl. Combine the soy sauce, mirin and ginger in a small bowl, pour over the chicken and toss until evenly coated. Marinate for at least 15 minutes, then drain off any excess marinade.

Mix the nori with the cornflour and, using your fingertips, lightly coat the chicken. Heat the oil in a deep-fryer or heavy-based saucepan to 180°C (350°F), or until a cube of bread dropped into the oil browns in 15 seconds. Fry 6–7 pieces of chicken at a time until golden, turning regularly. Drain on crumpled paper towels.

PREPARATION TIME: 25 MINUTES +   COOKING TIME: 20 MINUTES

Thai stuffed mussels

SAN CHOY BAU WITH NOODLES

500 g (1 lb 2 oz) raw prawns (shrimp),
vegetable oil, for deep-frying
100 g (3½ oz) dried rice vermicelli
(see Notes)
60 ml (2 fl oz/¼ cup) chicken stock
2 tablespoons Chinese rice wine
2 tablespoons soy sauce
2 tablespoons hoisin sauce
1 tablespoon brown bean sauce
½ teaspoon sugar
60 ml (2 fl oz/¼ cup) peanut oil
1 garlic clove, crushed
1 tablespoon finely chopped fresh ginger
3 spring onions (scallions), thinly sliced
and green ends reserved, to garnish
150 g (5½ oz) minced (ground) pork
(see Notes)
12 iceberg lettuce leaves, trimmed into
neat cups

SERVES 6

Peel the prawns and gently pull out the dark vein from each prawn back, starting at the head end. Roughly chop.

Fill a deep heavy-based saucepan or deep-fryer one-third full of oil and heat to 170°C (325°F), or until a cube of bread dropped into the oil browns in 20 seconds. Add the dried rice vermicelli to the oil in batches and deep-fry until puffed up but not browned — this will only take a few seconds, so watch it carefully. Remove with a slotted spoon and drain well on crumpled paper towels.

To make the stir-fry sauce, put the chicken stock, Chinese rice wine, soy sauce, hoisin sauce, brown bean sauce, sugar and ½ teaspoon salt in a small bowl and stir together until well combined.

Heat the peanut oil in a wok over high heat and swirl to coat. Add the garlic, ginger and spring onion and stir-fry for 1 minute, being careful not to burn the garlic.

Add the pork to the wok, breaking up the lumps with the back of a wooden spoon, then cook for 4 minutes. Add the prawn meat and stir-fry for 2 minutes, or until it begins to change colour.

Add the stir-fry sauce and stir until combined. Cook over high heat for 2 minutes, or until the mixture thickens slightly.

Divide the noodles among the lettuce cups, spoon the pork and prawn mixture over the noodles and garnish with the reserved spring onion. Serve at once.

PREPARATION TIME: 20 MINUTES   COOKING TIME: 15 MINUTES

NOTES: Make sure the pork mince is not too lean or the mixture will be dry. When deep-frying the vermicelli, take care not to allow the oil to become too hot or the noodles will expand and brown very quickly.
   Have everything you need ready before you start deep-frying — a slotted spoon for removing the noodles and a tray lined with crumpled paper towels. Remember to deep-fry the noodles in small batches as they will dramatically increase in volume when cooked.

ASIAN OYSTERS

12 oysters, on the shell
2 garlic cloves, finely chopped
2 x 2 cm (³/4 x ³/4 inch) piece fresh ginger,
cut into thin batons
2 spring onions (scallions), thinly sliced,
diagonally
60 ml (2 fl oz/¹/4 cup) Japanese soy sauce
60 ml (2 fl oz/¹/4 cup) peanut oil
coriander (cilantro) leaves, to garnish

SERVES 4

Line a large bamboo steamer with baking paper. Arrange the oysters in a single layer on top.

Put the garlic, ginger and spring onion in a bowl, mix together well, then sprinkle over the oysters. Spoon 1 teaspoon of soy sauce over each oyster. Cover and steam over a wok of simmering water for 2 minutes.

Heat the peanut oil in a small saucepan until smoking and carefully drizzle a little over each oyster. Garnish with the coriander leaves and serve immediately.

PREPARATION TIME: 15 MINUTES   COOKING TIME: 5 MINUTES

NOODLE-COATED PRAWNS

6 large raw prawns (shrimp)
¹/4 sheet nori
100 g (3¹/2 oz) somen noodles
oil, for deep-frying

BATTER
125 g (4¹/2 oz/1 cup) plain (all-purpose)
flour
1 egg yolk
250 ml (9 fl oz/1 cup) iced water

SOY AND GINGER SAUCE
1 tablespoon grated fresh ginger
2 teaspoons sugar
250 ml (9 fl oz/1 cup) soy sauce

SERVES 2

Peel the prawns, leaving the tails intact. Gently pull out the dark vein from each prawn back, starting at the head end. Make a shallow incision in the underside of the prawns and then open up the cut to straighten the prawns out. Cut the nori into strips about 7 cm (2³/4 inches) long and 1.5 cm (⁵/8 inch) wide. To make the batter, put the flour, egg yolk and water in a bowl and whisk until just combined. To make the sauce, combine all ingredients in a small bowl and mix well.

Break the noodles so that they are the same length as the prawns, not including the tails. Place the noodles on a board. Dip a prawn into the batter, then lay it, lengthways, on the noodles and gather up the noodles to cover the prawns all around. Press so they stick to the prawn. Wrap a strip of nori around the centre of the prawn, dampen the ends with a little water and press to seal. Repeat with the rest of the prawns.

Fill a deep-fryer or heavy-based saucepan one-third full of oil and heat to 170°C (325°F), or until a cube of bread dropped into the oil browns in 20 seconds. Cook the prawn bundles in two batches, until the noodles are golden brown. Serve immediately with the sauce.

PREPARATION TIME: 20 MINUTES   COOKING TIME: 15 MINUTES

PEKING DUCK WITH MANDARIN PANCAKES

1.7 kg (3 lb 12 oz) duck, washed
3 litres (104 fl oz/12 cups) boiling water
1 tablespoon honey
12 spring onions (scallions)
1 Lebanese (short) cucumber, seeded
and cut into batons
2 tablespoons hoisin sauce

MANDARIN PANCAKES
310 g (11 oz/2$^1/2$ cups) plain
(all-purpose) flour
2 teaspoons caster (superfine) sugar
250 ml (9 fl oz/1 cup) boiling water
1 tablespoon sesame oil

SERVES 6

Remove the neck and any large pieces of fat from inside the duck carcass. Hold the duck over the sink and very carefully and slowly pour the boiling water over it, rotating the duck so the water scalds all the skin. Put the duck on a rack in an ovenproof dish. Mix the honey and 125 ml (4 fl oz/$^1/2$ cup) hot water and brush two coats of this glaze all over the duck. Dry the duck in a cool, airy place for about 4 hours. The skin is sufficiently dry when it feels papery.

Preheat the oven to 210°C (415°F/Gas 6–7). Cut an 8 cm (3$^1/4$ inch) section from the white end of each spring onion. Make fine parallel cuts from the top of the section towards the white end. Put the onion pieces in iced water — they will open into 'brushes'. Roast the duck for 30 minutes, then turn it over carefully without tearing the skin and roast it for another 30 minutes. Remove the duck from the oven and leave for a minute or two, then place it on a warm dish.

Meanwhile, to make the pancakes, put the flour and sugar in a bowl and pour in the boiling water. Stir the mixture a few times and leave until lukewarm. Knead the mixture, on a lightly floured surface, into a smooth dough. Cover and set aside for 30 minutes. Take two level tablespoons of dough and roll each one into a ball. Roll out to circles 8 cm (3$^1/4$ inches) in diameter. Lightly brush one of the circles with sesame oil and place the other circle on top. Re-roll to make a thin pancake about 15 cm (6 inches) in diameter. Repeat with the remaining dough and oil to make about 10 'double' pancakes.

Heat a frying pan and cook the pancakes one at a time. When small bubbles appear on the surface, turn the pancake over and cook the second side, pressing the surface with a clean tea towel (dish towel). The pancake should puff up when done. Transfer the pancake to a plate. When cool enough to handle, peel the two halves of the double pancake apart. Stack them on a plate and cover them at once to prevent them drying out.

To serve, thinly slice the duck. Place the pancakes and duck on separate serving plates. Arrange the cucumber sticks and spring onion brushes on another serving plate. Put the hoisin sauce in a small dish. Each diner helps themselves to a pancake, spreads a little sauce on it and adds a couple of pieces of cucumber, a spring onion brush and, finally, a piece of duck. The pancake is then folded over into a neat envelope for eating.

PREPARATION TIME: 1 HOUR +   COOKING TIME: 1 HOUR 15 MINUTES

STUFFED PRAWN OMELETTES

500 g (1 lb 2 oz) raw prawns (shrimp)
1½ tablespoons oil
4 eggs, lightly beaten
2 tablespoons fish sauce
8 spring onions (scallions), chopped
6 coriander (cilantro) roots, chopped
2 garlic cloves, chopped
1 small red chilli, seeded and chopped
2 teaspoons lime juice
2 teaspoons grated palm sugar (jaggery) or soft brown sugar
3 tablespoons chopped coriander (cilantro) leaves
1 small red chilli, extra, chopped to garnish
coriander (cilantro) sprigs, to garnish
sweet chilli sauce, to serve

MAKES 8

Peel the prawns, gently pull out the dark vein from each prawn back, starting from the head end, then chop the prawn meat.

Heat a wok over high heat, add 2 teaspoons of the oil and swirl to coat. Combine the egg with half of the fish sauce. Add 2 tablespoons of the mixture to the wok and swirl to a 16 cm (6¼ inch) round. Cook for 1 minute, then gently lift out. Repeat with the remaining egg mixture to make eight omelettes.

Heat the remaining oil in the wok. Add the prawns, spring onion, coriander root, garlic and chilli. Stir-fry for 3–4 minutes, or until the prawns are cooked. Stir in the lime juice, palm sugar, coriander leaves and the remaining fish sauce.

Divide the prawn mixture among the omelettes and fold each into a small firm parcel. Cut a slit in the top and garnish with the chilli and coriander sprigs. Serve with sweet chilli sauce.

PREPARATION TIME: 25 MINUTES   COOKING TIME: 15 MINUTES

CHINESE BROCCOLI WITH GINGER, LIME AND PEANUTS

40 g (1½ oz) tamarind pulp
60 ml (2 fl oz/¼ cup) boiling water
1 tablespoon peanut oil
600 g (1 lb 5 oz) Chinese broccoli, trimmed and halved widthways
1 small red chilli, seeded and finely chopped
2 garlic cloves, finely chopped
3 teaspoons finely grated fresh ginger
1 tablespoon sugar
1 tablespoon lime juice
1 teaspoon sesame oil
1 tablespoon roasted unsalted peanuts, finely chopped

SERVES 4

Put the tamarind pulp in a bowl and pour in the boiling water. Allow to steep for 5 minutes, then strain. Discard the solids.

Heat a non-stick wok over high heat, add the peanut oil and swirl to coat. Add the Chinese broccoli and stir-fry for 2–3 minutes, or until wilted. Add the chilli, garlic and ginger and cook for another minute, then add the sugar, lime juice and 1 tablespoon of the tamarind liquid and simmer for 1 minute. Transfer to a plate and drizzle with the sesame oil. Scatter with peanuts, then serve.

PREPARATION TIME: 5 MINUTES +   COOKING TIME: 5 MINUTES

BRAISED BOK CHOY

2 tablespoons peanut oil
1 garlic clove, crushed
1 tablespoon fresh ginger, cut into thin batons
500 g (1 lb 2 oz) bok choy (pak choy), separated, cut into 8 cm (3¼ inch) lengths
1 teaspoon sugar
1 teaspoon sesame oil
1 tablespoon oyster sauce

SERVES 4

Heat a wok over high heat, add the oil and swirl to coat. Add the garlic and ginger and stir-fry for 1–2 minutes. Add the bok choy and stir-fry for 1 minute. Add the sugar, a pinch of salt and pepper and 60 ml (2 fl oz/¼ cup) water. Bring to the boil, then reduce the heat and simmer, covered, for 3 minutes, or until the stems are tender but crisp.

Stir in the sesame oil and oyster sauce and serve immediately.

PREPARATION TIME: 10 MINUTES   COOKING TIME: 5 MINUTES

Chinese broccoli with ginger, lime and peanuts

MARINATED TOFU

2 lemon grass stems, white part only
1 small red chilli
500 g (1 lb 2 oz) fried tofu puffs
125 ml (4 fl oz/½ cup) peanut oil
2 garlic cloves, crushed
1 teaspoon grated fresh ginger
2 tablespoons fish sauce
2 tablespoons lime juice
1 tablespoon soft brown sugar
oil, for frying

SERVES 4

Finely chop the lemon grass and chilli. Cut the tofu puffs diagonally in half.

Combine all the ingredients except the frying oil in a flat non-metallic dish. Toss the tofu until it is completely coated in the marinade, then cover with plastic wrap and refrigerate overnight.

Heat a lightly oiled wok over high heat and stir-fry the tofu in batches for 1–2 minutes, or until browned. Serve hot.

PREPARATION TIME: 10 MINUTES +   COOKING TIME: 15 MINUTES

RED COOKED PORK BELLY

6 dried shiitake mushrooms

250 ml (9 fl oz/1 cup) boiling water

2 teaspoons peanut oil

1 kg (2 lb 4 oz) piece pork belly

500 ml (17 fl oz/2 cups) chicken stock

60 ml (2 fl oz/¼ cup) dark soy sauce

60 ml (2 fl oz/¼ cup) Chinese rice wine

4 garlic cloves, bruised

5 x 5 cm (2 x 2 inch) piece fresh ginger, sliced

1 piece dried mandarin or tangerine peel

2 teaspoons sichuan peppercorns

2 star anise

1 cinnamon stick

1½ tablespoons Chinese rock sugar (see Note)

Thai basil sprigs, to garnish

SERVES 6

Cover the mushrooms in the boiling water and soak for 20 minutes, or until soft. Squeeze dry, reserving the liquid.

Heat a large wok over high heat, add the oil and swirl to coat. Add the pork, skin side down, and cook for 5 minutes, or until well browned, then turn over and cook for a further 6 minutes, or until sealed.

Add the stock, soy sauce, rice wine, garlic, ginger, citrus peel, spices, reserved mushroom soaking liquid and 500 ml (17 fl oz/2 cups) water. Bring to the boil, then reduce the heat to low and simmer, covered, for 1¼ hours.

Add the sugar and mushrooms and cook for a further 45 minutes, or until the pork is very tender. Remove the pork from the stock and cut into slices about 1 cm (½ inch) thick. Strain the liquid into a bowl, then return the strained liquid to the wok. Bring to the boil and continue boiling until reduced to about 185 ml (6 fl oz/¾ cup).

Place the pork on a platter with the mushrooms and spoon on some of the cooking liquid. Garnish with the Thai basil. Serve with steamed rice.

PREPARATION TIME: 10 MINUTES +   COOKING TIME: 2 HOURS 10 MINUTES

NOTE: Chinese rock sugar is the crystallized form of saturated sugar liquor. It is named for its irregular rock-shaped pieces and imparts a rich flavour, especially to braised or 'red cooked' foods as well as sweets, glazing them with a translucent sheen. Available in the Asian section of large supermarkets, or in Asian grocery stores.

CHU CHEE SEAFOOD CURRY

500 g (1 lb 2 oz) raw king prawns (shrimp)
500 g (1 lb 2 oz) scallops, without roe
two 270 ml (9½ fl oz) tins coconut cream
(do not shake)
55 g (2 oz/¼ cup) chu chee curry paste
(see Note)
2–3 tablespoons fish sauce
2–3 tablespoons grated palm sugar
(jaggery) or soft brown sugar
8 makrut (kaffir lime) leaves, finely
shredded
2 small red chillies, thinly sliced (optional)
1 very large handful Thai basil

SERVES 4

Peel the prawns, leaving the tails intact. Gently pull out the dark vein from each prawn back, starting at the head end. Remove and discard any veins, membrane or hard white muscle from the scallops.

Lift off the thick cream from the top of the coconut cream — there should be about 250 ml (9 fl oz/1 cup) of cream — and put it in a wok. Bring to the boil, then stir in the curry paste. Reduce the heat and simmer for 10 minutes, or until fragrant and the oil begins to separate from the cream.

Stir in the seafood and remaining coconut cream and cook for 5 minutes. Add the fish sauce, sugar, makrut (kaffir lime) leaves and chilli and cook for 1 minute. Stir in half the basil and use the rest to garnish.

PREPARATION TIME: 20 MINUTES COOKING TIME: 20 MINUTES

NOTE: Chu chee curry paste can be bought from Asian food speciality stores.

SCALLOPS WITH BLACK BEAN SAUCE

600 g (1 lb 5 oz) large scallops,
without roe
2 tablespoons cornflour (cornstarch)
80 ml (2½ fl oz/⅓ cup) peanut oil
3 spring onions (scallions), cut into 3 cm
(1¼ inch) lengths
1 teaspoon finely chopped fresh ginger
2 garlic cloves, crushed
2 tablespoons Chinese rice wine
55 g (2 oz/¼ cup) black beans, rinsed
and roughly chopped
1 tablespoon rice vinegar
1 tablespoon soy sauce
1 teaspoon soft brown sugar
½ teaspoon sesame oil

SERVES 4–6

Remove and discard any veins, membrane or hard white muscle from the scallops. Toss them in the cornflour to coat, then shake off any excess.

Heat a wok over high heat, add 1 teaspoon of the peanut oil and swirl to coat. Add the spring onion and stir-fry for 30 seconds. Remove from the wok. Add 1 tablespoon of the peanut oil to the hot wok, then add one-third of the scallops and stir-fry for 1–2 minutes, or until golden and well sealed — no liquid should be released. Remove from the wok. Repeat with the rest of the scallops.

Add the remaining peanut oil to the wok and swirl to coat. Add the ginger, garlic, rice wine, beans, vinegar, soy sauce and sugar, and stir-fry for 1 minute, or until the sauce thickens slightly. Return the scallops to the wok and stir-fry for 1 minute, or until heated through and the sauce has thickened again. Stir in the spring onion and sesame oil. Serve with steamed rice.

PREPARATION TIME: 15 MINUTES COOKING TIME: 10 MINUTES

Chu chee seafood curry

HAINANESE CHICKEN RICE

2 kg (4 lb 8 oz) chicken
6 spring onions (scallions)
a few thick slices fresh ginger
4 garlic cloves, bruised
1 teaspoon vegetable oil
1 teaspoon sesame oil

RICE

5 red Asian shallots, finely chopped
2 garlic cloves, crushed
1 tablespoon very finely chopped
fresh ginger
300 g (10½ oz/1½ cups) jasmine rice
100 g (3½ oz/½ cup) long-grain
glutinous rice
3 roma (plum) tomatoes, cut into
thin wedges
3 Lebanese (short) cucumbers,
sliced diagonally
coriander (cilantro) sprigs, to garnish

SAUCE

2 small red chillies, seeded and chopped
4 garlic cloves, roughly chopped
1½ tablespoons finely chopped
fresh ginger
3 coriander (cilantro) roots, chopped
2 tablespoons dark soy sauce
2 tablespoons lime juice
2 tablespoons sugar
pinch ground white pepper

SERVES 6

Remove the excess fat from around the cavity of the chicken and reserve. Rinse and salt the inside of the chicken and rinse again. Insert the spring onions, ginger slices and garlic into the chicken cavity then place, breast side down, in a large saucepan and cover with cold water. Add 1 teaspoon salt and bring to the boil over high heat, skimming the surface as required. Reduce the heat to low and simmer gently for 15 minutes, then carefully turn over without piercing the skin and cook for another 15 minutes, or until the thigh juices run clear when pierced.

Carefully lift the chicken out of the saucepan, draining any liquid from the cavity into the rest of the stock. Reserve 1 litre (35 fl oz/4 cups) of the stock. Plunge the chicken into iced water for 5 minutes to stop the cooking process and to firm the skin. Rub the entire surface of the chicken with the combined vegetable and sesame oils and allow to cool while you make the rice.

To make the rice, cook the reserved chicken fat in a saucepan over medium heat for about 8 minutes, or until you have about 2 tablespoons of liquid fat, then discard the solids. (If you prefer, use vegetable oil instead.) Add the shallots and cook for a few minutes, or until lightly golden, then add the garlic and ginger and stir until fragrant. Add both the rices and cook for 5 minutes, or until lightly golden, then pour in the reserved chicken stock and 1 teaspoon salt and bring to the boil. Cover and reduce the heat to low and cook for about 20 minutes, or until tender and the liquid has evaporated. Cool, covered, for 10 minutes, then fluff with a fork.

Meanwhile, to make the sauce, pound the chillies, garlic, ginger and coriander roots into a paste using a mortar and pestle. Stir in the rest of the ingredients and season to taste.

Shred the chicken. Divide the rice into six slightly wetted Chinese soup bowls and press down firmly, then turn out onto serving plates. Serve the pieces of chicken on a platter with the tomato, cucumber and coriander and pour the dipping sauce into a small bowl or individual sauce dishes and let your guests help themselves.

PREPARATION TIME: 50 MINUTES +   COOKING TIME: 1 HOUR 30 MINUTES

SQUID WITH GREEN PEPPERCORNS

600 g (1 lb 5 oz) squid tubes, washed and dried
2 teaspoons chopped coriander (cilantro) root
3 garlic cloves, crushed
80 ml (2¹/₂ fl oz/¹/₃ cup) oil
25 g (1 oz) Thai green peppercorns on the stalk, in brine, or lightly crushed fresh peppercorns
2 tablespoons Thai mushroom soy sauce
¹/₂ teaspoon grated palm sugar (jaggery) or soft brown sugar
1 large handful Thai basil

SERVES 4

Cut the squid tubes in half lengthways. Clean and remove the quills. Score a diamond pattern on the inside of the squid. Cut into 4 cm (1¹/₂ inch) square pieces.

Put the coriander root, 1 garlic clove and 1 tablespoon of the oil in a food processor and process to form a smooth paste. Mix together the paste and squid pieces, cover and marinate in the fridge for 30 minutes.

Heat a wok over high heat, add the remaining oil and swirl to coat. Add the squid pieces and the remaining garlic and stir-fry for 1 minute. Add the peppercorns and stir-fry for a further 2 minutes, or until the squid is just cooked — it will toughen if overcooked. Add the soy sauce and palm sugar, and stir until the sugar has dissolved. Serve immediately, garnished with Thai basil.

PREPARATION TIME: 10 MINUTES +   COOKING TIME: 5 MINUTES

JASMINE TEA STEAMED FISH

200 g (7 oz) jasmine tea leaves
100 g (3¹/₂ oz) fresh ginger, thinly sliced
4 spring onions (scallions), cut into 5 cm (2 inch) lengths
4 x 200 g (7 oz) skinless firm white fish fillets

GINGER SPRING ONION SAUCE
125 ml (4 fl oz/¹/₂ cup) fish stock
60 ml (2 fl oz/¹/₄ cup) light soy sauce
3 spring onions (scallions), thinly sliced
1 tablespoon finely shredded fresh ginger
2 teaspoons sugar
1 large red chilli, sliced

SERVES 4

Line a double bamboo steamer with baking paper. Place the tea, ginger and spring onion in a layer on the bottom steamer basket. Cover and steam over a wok of simmering water for 10 minutes, or until the tea is moist and fragrant.

Lay the fish in a single layer in the top steamer basket and steam for 5–10 minutes, or until the fish flakes easily when tested with a fork.

To make the sauce, combine all the ingredients in a small saucepan with 125 ml (4 fl oz/¹/₂ cup) water. Heat over low heat for 5 minutes, or until the sugar has dissolved. Drizzle the fish with the sauce and serve with rice.

PREPARATION TIME: 10 MINUTES   COOKING TIME: 25 MINUTES

Squid with green peppercorns

BAKED FISH WITH NOODLE FILLING

2 kg (4 lb 8 oz) ocean trout or 1 whole
salmon, boned and butterflied
(see Note)
100 g (3½ oz) rice stick noodles
1 tablespoon peanut oil
6 red Asian shallots, chopped
2 red chillies, chopped
2 tablespoons grated fresh ginger
200 g (7 oz) water chestnuts, chopped
200 g (7 oz) bamboo shoots, chopped
6 spring onions (scallions), sliced
2 tablespoons chopped coriander
(cilantro) root
3 tablespoons chopped coriander
(cilantro) leaves
2 tablespoons fish sauce
2 tablespoons grated palm sugar
(jaggery) or soft brown sugar

LIME BUTTER SAUCE
4 makrut (kaffir lime) leaves, finely
shredded
2 tablespoons lime juice
125 g (4½ oz) butter

SERVES 10–12

Preheat the oven to 180°C (350°F/Gas 4). Pat the fish dry and use tweezers to remove any remaining small bones.

Soak the noodles in boiling water for 10 minutes. Drain well, pat dry and cut into short lengths.

Heat the oil in a frying pan and cook the shallots, chilli and ginger over medium heat for about 5 minutes, or until the shallots are golden. Transfer to a bowl. Add the noodles, water chestnuts, bamboo shoots, spring onion, coriander root and leaves, fish sauce and palm sugar to the bowl and mix well.

Open the trout or salmon fillet out flat and spread the noodle filling over the centre. Fold the fish over to enclose the filling and secure with string every 5 cm (2 inches) along the fish. Place onto a baking tray lined with foil and bake for 30–40 minutes, or until tender.

To make the sauce, put the makrut (kaffir lime) leaves, lime juice and butter in a saucepan and cook over medium heat until the butter turns nutty brown. Cut the salmon into slices, discarding the string, then serve topped with the sauce.

PREPARATION TIME: 20 MINUTES +   COOKING TIME: 50 MINUTES

NOTE: A fish that has been butterflied has been carefully slit through the middle, along the bones, but not all the way through. The effect is of having a hinge on one side of the fish. Another term for this is 'pocket boning'. Ask your fishmonger to do this for you.

THAI DUCK AND PINEAPPLE CURRY

1 tablespoon peanut oil
8 spring onions (scallions), sliced diagonally into 3 cm (1¼ inch) lengths
2 garlic cloves, crushed
2–4 tablespoons Thai red curry paste
750 g (1 lb 10 oz) Chinese roast duck, chopped
400 ml (14 fl oz) coconut milk
450 g (1 lb) tinned pineapple pieces in syrup, drained
3 makrut (kaffir lime) leaves
3 tablespoons chopped coriander (cilantro) leaves
2 tablespoons chopped mint

SERVES 4–6

Heat a wok until very hot, add the oil and swirl to coat. Add the spring onion, garlic and red curry paste, and stir-fry for 1 minute, or until fragrant.

Add the duck pieces, coconut milk, pineapple pieces, makrut (kaffir lime) leaves, and half the coriander and mint. Bring to the boil, then reduce the heat and simmer for 10 minutes, or until the duck is heated through and the sauce has thickened slightly. Stir in the remaining coriander and mint, and serve with jasmine rice.

PREPARATION TIME: 10 MINUTES   COOKING TIME: 15 MINUTES

ASIAN PEPPERED BEEF

2 onions, thinly sliced
2 garlic cloves, finely chopped
2 teaspoons finely chopped fresh ginger
2 tablespoons Chinese rice wine
1 tablespoon soy sauce
1 tablespoon oyster sauce
2 teaspoons sugar
1 teaspoon sesame oil
1 teaspoon sichuan peppercorns, crushed
1 tablespoon black peppercorns, crushed
600 g (1 lb 5 oz) lean beef fillet, thinly sliced across the grain
2 spring onions (scallions), cut into 2.5 cm (1 inch) lengths
2 tablespoons vegetable oil

SERVES 4

Combine the onion, garlic, ginger, rice wine, soy sauce, oyster sauce, sugar, sesame oil and peppercorns in a non-metallic bowl. Add the beef, cover and marinate in the refrigerator for at least 2 hours.

Drain the beef, discarding any excess liquid, then stir in the spring onion.

Heat a wok over high heat, add half the oil and swirl to coat. Add half the beef and stir-fry for 6 minutes, or until seared and cooked to your liking. Repeat with the remaining oil and beef. Serve with steamed rice.

PREPARATION TIME: 10 MINUTES +   COOKING TIME: 15 MINUTES

Thai duck and pineapple curry

SINGAPORE PEPPER CRAB

2 kg (4 lb 8 oz) fresh blue swimmer crabs
2 tablespoons dark soy sauce
2 tablespoons oyster sauce
1 tablespoon grated palm sugar (jaggery)
or soft brown sugar
1–2 tablespoons peanut oil
150 g (5½ oz) butter
2 tablespoons finely chopped garlic
1 tablespoon finely chopped fresh ginger
1 small red chilli, seeded and finely
chopped
1½ tablespoons ground black pepper
1 spring onion (scallion), green part only,
thinly sliced, diagonally
lemon slices, to serve

SERVES 4

Wash the crabs well with a stiff brush. Pull back the apron and remove the top shell from each crab (it should come off easily and in one piece). Remove the intestine and the grey feathery gills. Using a large sharp knife, cut the crab lengthways through the centre of the body, to form two halves with the legs attached. Cut each half in half again, crossways. Crack the thicker part of the legs with the back of a heavy knife or crab crackers to allow the flavour to get into the meat and make it easier for your guests to break them open.

To make the stir-fry sauce, combine the soy sauce, oyster sauce and palm sugar in a small bowl. Set aside until needed.

Heat a wok over high heat, add 1 tablespoon of the oil and swirl to coat. Add the crab pieces in a few batches, stir-frying over very high heat for 4 minutes each batch, or until the shells turn bright orange all over, adding a little more oil if needed. Remove from the wok.

Reduce the heat to medium–high, add the butter, garlic, ginger, chilli and pepper and stir-fry for 30 seconds, or until fragrant, then add the stir-fry sauce and simmer for a further minute, or until glossy.

Return the crab to the wok, cover and stir every minute for 4 minutes, or until the crab is cooked. Sprinkle with the spring onion and serve immediately with rice. Put small bowls of warm water with lemon slices on the table for rinsing sticky fingers.

PREPARATION TIME: 15 MINUTES +   COOKING TIME: 20 MINUTES

NOTE: This dish is very rich and best served as part of a banquet. In Singapore, crab is served with paper bibs as it is very messy to eat — a paper towel or serviette will do just as well.

CHICKEN, THAI BASIL AND CASHEW STIR-FRY

750 g (1 lb 10 oz) boneless, skinless chicken breast, cut into strips
2 lemon grass stems, white part only, finely chopped
3 small red chillies, seeded and chopped
4 garlic cloves, crushed
1 tablespoon finely chopped fresh ginger
2 coriander (cilantro) roots, finely chopped
2 tablespoons oil
100 g (3½ oz/⅔ cup) cashew nuts
1½ tablespoons lime juice
2 tablespoons fish sauce
1½ tablespoons grated palm sugar (jaggery) or soft brown sugar
2 very large handfuls Thai basil
2 teaspoons cornflour (cornstarch)

SERVES 4

Put the chicken in a large bowl with the lemon grass, chilli, garlic, ginger and coriander root. Mix together well.

Heat a wok over medium heat, add 1 teaspoon of the oil and swirl to coat. Add the cashews and cook for 1 minute, or until lightly golden. Remove and drain on crumpled paper towels.

Heat the remaining oil in the wok, add the chicken in batches and stir-fry over medium heat for 4–5 minutes, or until browned. Return the chicken to the wok.

Stir in the lime juice, fish sauce, palm sugar and basil, and cook for 30–60 seconds, or until the basil just begins to wilt. Mix the cornflour with 1 tablespoon water, add to the wok and stir until the mixture thickens slightly. Stir in the cashews and serve with steamed rice.

PREPARATION TIME: 15 MINUTES   COOKING TIME: 15 MINUTES

CHICKEN BRAISED WITH GINGER AND STAR ANISE

1 teaspoon sichuan peppercorns
2 tablespoons peanut oil
2 x 3 cm (¾ x 1¼ inch) piece fresh ginger, cut into thin batons
2 garlic cloves, chopped
1 kg (2 lb 4 oz) boneless, skinless chicken thighs, halved
80 ml (2½ fl oz/⅓ cup) Chinese rice wine
1 tablespoon honey
60 ml (2 fl oz/¼ cup) light soy sauce
1 star anise

SERVES 4

Heat a wok over medium heat, add the peppercorns and cook, stirring often, for 2–4 minutes, or until fragrant. Remove and lightly crush with the back of a knife.

Reheat the wok, add the oil and swirl to coat. Add the ginger and garlic and cook over low heat for 1–2 minutes, or until lightly golden. Add the chicken, increase the heat to medium and cook for 3 minutes, or until browned all over.

Add the remaining ingredients, reduce the heat and simmer, covered, for 20 minutes, or until the chicken is tender. Serve with rice.

PREPARATION TIME: 10 MINUTES   COOKING TIME: 30 MINUTES

Chicken, Thai basil and cashew stir-fry

STICKY RICE WITH MANGOES

400 g (14 oz/2 cups) glutinous white rice
1 tablespoon white sesame seeds
250 ml (9 fl oz/1 cup) coconut milk
70 g (2$\frac{1}{2}$ oz/$\frac{1}{2}$ cup) grated palm sugar
(jaggery) or soft brown sugar
2–3 mangoes, peeled, stoned and sliced
60 ml (2 fl oz/$\frac{1}{4}$ cup) coconut cream
mint sprigs, to garnish

SERVES 4

Put the rice in a sieve and wash it under running water until the water runs clear. Put the rice in a glass or ceramic bowl, cover it with water and leave it to soak overnight, or for a minimum of 12 hours. Drain the rice.

Line a metal or bamboo steamer with muslin (cheesecloth). Place the rice on top of the muslin and cover the steamer with a tight-fitting lid. Place the steamer over a saucepan of boiling water and steam over medium–low heat for 50 minutes, or until the rice is cooked. Transfer the rice to a large bowl and fluff it up with a fork.

Toast the sesame seeds in a dry frying pan over medium heat for 3–4 minutes, shaking the pan gently, until the seeds are golden brown. Remove from the pan at once to prevent burning.

Pour the coconut milk into a small saucepan, then add the sugar and $\frac{1}{4}$ teaspoon salt. Slowly bring the mixture to the boil, stirring constantly until the sugar has dissolved. Reduce the heat and simmer for 5 minutes, or until the mixture has thickened slightly. Stir the mixture often while it is simmering, and take care that it does not stick to the bottom of the pan.

Slowly pour the coconut milk over the top of the rice. Use a fork to lift and fluff the rice. Do not stir the liquid through, otherwise the rice will become too gluggy. Let the rice mixture rest for 20 minutes before carefully spooning it into the centre of four warmed serving plates. Arrange the mango slices around the rice mounds. Spoon a little coconut cream over the rice, sprinkle with the sesame seeds, and garnish with the mint leaves.

PREPARATION TIME: 40 MINUTES +   COOKING TIME: 1 HOUR

BANANA AND COCONUT PANCAKES

1 tablespoon shredded coconut
40 g (1½ oz/⅓ cup) plain (all-purpose) flour
2 tablespoons rice flour
55 g (2 oz/¼ cup) caster (superfine) sugar
25 g (1 oz/¼ cup) desiccated coconut
250 ml (9 fl oz/1 cup) coconut milk
1 egg, lightly beaten
butter, for frying
60 g (2¼ oz) butter, extra
4 large bananas, cut diagonally into thick slices
60 g (2¼ oz/⅓ cup) lightly packed soft brown sugar
80 ml (2½ fl oz/⅓ cup) lime juice
shredded lime zest, to serve

SERVES 4–6

Spread the shredded coconut on a baking tray and toast it in a 150°C (300°F/Gas 2) oven for 10 minutes, or until it is dark golden, shaking the tray occasionally. Remove from the tray and set aside. Sift the flours into a bowl. Add the sugar and desiccated coconut and mix. Make a well in the centre, pour in the combined coconut milk and egg, and beat until smooth.

Melt a little butter in a non-stick frying pan. Pour 60 ml (2 fl oz/¼ cup) of the pancake mixture into the pan and cook over medium heat until the underside is golden. Turn the pancake over and cook the other side. Transfer to a plate and cover with a tea towel (dish towel) to keep warm. Repeat with the remaining pancake batter, buttering the pan when necessary.

Heat the extra butter in the pan, add the banana, toss until coated, and cook over medium heat until the banana starts to soften and brown. Sprinkle with the brown sugar and shake the pan gently until the sugar has melted. Stir in the lime juice. Divide the banana among the pancakes and fold over to enclose. Sprinkle with the toasted coconut and shredded lime zest.

PREPARATION TIME: 10 MINUTES   COOKING TIME: 30 MINUTES

COCONUT ICE CREAM

435 ml (15¼ fl oz/1¾ cups) coconut cream
375 ml (13 fl oz/1½ cups) pouring (whipping) cream
2 eggs
2 egg yolks
115 g (4 oz/½ cup) caster (superfine) sugar
1 teaspoon natural vanilla extract
15 g (½ oz/¼ cup) shredded coconut, toasted (see recipe above)
mint, to garnish

SERVES 6

Stir the coconut cream and cream in a saucepan over medium heat without boiling for 2–3 minutes. Remove from the heat, cover and keep warm. Put the eggs, yolks, sugar, vanilla and ¼ teaspoon salt in a large heatproof bowl. Using electric beaters, beat the mixture for 2–3 minutes until frothy and thick. Put the bowl over a saucepan of simmering water. Beat, then gradually add the cream mixture, 60 ml (2 fl oz/¼ cup) at a time, for 10 minutes, or until all the cream mixture is added and the custard has thickened to the consistency of thin cream. Do not allow it to boil. Transfer to a cold bowl, cover and leave to cool, stirring occasionally

Transfer to an ice cream machine and freeze according to manufacturer's instructions. Alternatively, transfer to a shallow metal tray and freeze, whisking every couple of hours until frozen and creamy. Freeze for 5 hours or overnight. Soften in the fridge for 30 minutes before serving in scoops with the coconut sprinkled over and garnished with the mint.

PREPARATION TIME: 10 MINUTES +   COOKING TIME: 15 MINUTES

Banana and coconut pancakes

INDEX

INDEX